TO

Mom

FROM

Your only son

DATE

*May 9th, Happy Mother's Day
2021*

FROM GRITS TO Grace

DEVOTIONS
FROM THE
FARMHOUSE PORCH

Criswell Freeman (quotedoctor@comcast.net or 615-665-9972)

Cover Design: Jessica Wei

Contents

A Message to Readers from the Front Porch

Because you've picked up a devotional book with the word "Grits" in its title, you probably have more than a passing interest in both old-time religion and down-home country wisdom. If so, you've come to the right place. On the pages that follow, you'll be treated to a collection of timely wisdom, timeless scripture, classic hymns, inspirational poems, and daily devotionals. And as you read along day by day, you'll discover a dash of down-home country humor, too.

In rural America, the Christian faith has been expressed for centuries through song and verse. Today, the gospel message remains near and dear to millions of believers who still enjoy the simple pleasures of a quiet evening spent talking and rocking on the front porch. The ideas in this book remind us that God's grace is free, that His love endures forever, and that His faithfulness extends to good ol' boys and city folk alike.

The Bible is a book like no other. It is a gift from the Creator, an instruction book for life here on Earth and a roadmap for life eternal. And it's a book of promises. When God makes a promise, He keeps it. No exceptions. So the verses in this text are not hypotheticals; they're certainties. They apply to every generation, to every nationality, and to every corner of the globe, including yours. And His promises apply to every human being, including you.

If you're ready for a heaping helping of inspiration and truth, keep reading. When you do, you'll discover that old-time religion has never gone out of style...and never will.

Amazing Grace

JOHN NEWTON
1779

Amazing grace! How sweet the sound
That saved a wretch like me!
I once was lost, but now am found;
Was blind, but now I see.

'Twas grace that taught my heart to fear,
And grace my fears relieved;
How precious did that grace appear
The hour I first believed.

Through many dangers, toils and snares,
I have already come;
'Tis grace hath brought me safe thus far,
And grace will lead me home.

When we've been there ten thousand years,
Bright shining as the sun,
We've no less days to sing God's praise
Than when we'd first begun.

Grits to Grace

For you are saved by grace through faith,
and this is not from yourselves; it is God's gift—
not from works, so that no one can boast.

EPHESIANS 2:8–9 HCSB

Whether you're on the front porch, the back porch, or anyplace else, for that matter, God is with you. Whether you're enjoying a big country breakfast, a simple picnic lunch, or an old-fashioned barbeque cookout, God is right there, always ready to guide your steps and hear your prayers. Whether your style is country-fried or citified, high-fashion or no-fashion, grits or gourmet, God's grace is absolutely free for the asking, paid for in full. No shoes, no shirt, no problem—He loves you just as you are.

John Newton had already experienced God's transforming power when he penned "Amazing Grace," which is not only one of the most recognizable hymns in the English language, but also a favorite in small-town country churches from sea to shining sea. The hymn's message is as fresh today as it was on that day it was written. Newton understood that God's grace is sufficient to meet our every need. And, we should understand it, too.

No matter our circumstances, no matter our personal histories, no matter our frailties and faults, the Lord loves us. Since all of us are sinners, we all need His grace. And when we entrust our hearts and lives to the Him, we can rest assured that He will pilot us safely home. Amazing.

God is the giver, and we are the receivers.
And His richest gifts are bestowed not upon those
who do the greatest things, but upon those
who accept His abundance and His grace.

HANNAH WHITALL SMITH

MORE FROM GOD'S WORD

But because of his great love for us, God,
who is rich in mercy, made us alive with Christ
even when we were dead in transgressions—
it is by grace you have been saved.

EPHESIANS 2:4–5 NIV

But grow in the grace and knowledge of our Lord
and Savior Jesus Christ. To Him be the glory,
both now and to the day of eternity.

2 PETER 3:18 NASB

We have redemption in Him through His blood,
the forgiveness of our trespasses, according to
the riches of His grace that He lavished on us
with all wisdom and understanding.

EPHESIANS 1:7–8 HCSB

My grace is sufficient for you,
for my power is made perfect in weakness.

2 CORINTHIANS 12:9 NIV

But he gives us more grace. That is why Scripture says:
"God opposes the proud but gives grace to the humble."

JAMES 4:6 NIV

The well of
God's forgiveness

never

runs

dry.

—GRADY NUTT

The Old Rugged Cross

GEORGE BENNARD
1915

On a hill far away stood an old rugged cross,
The emblem of suffering and shame;
And I love that old cross where the dearest and best
For a world of lost sinners was slain.

REFRAIN
So I'll cherish the old rugged cross,
Till my trophies at last I lay down;
I will cling to the old rugged cross,
And exchange it some day for a crown.

O that old rugged cross, so despised by the world,
Has a wondrous attraction for me;
For the dear Lamb of God left his glory above
To bear it to dark Calvary.

To that old rugged cross I will ever be true,
Its shame and reproach gladly bear;
Then he'll call me some day to my home far away,
Where his glory forever I'll share.

On a Hill Far Away

I am the good shepherd.
The good shepherd lays down his life for the sheep.
JOHN 10:11 NIV

On a rugged cross, on a faraway hill, Jesus was crucified. At noon, darkness came over the land; the curtain of the temple was torn in two; and finally Jesus called out, "'Father, into Your hands I commit My spirit.' Having said this, He breathed His last." (Luke 23:46 NKJV). Christ had endured the crucifixion, and it was finished.

The body was wrapped in a linen shroud and placed in a new tomb. It was there that God breathed life into His Son. It was there that Christ was resurrected. It was there that the angels rejoiced. And it was there that God's plan for the salvation of mankind was made complete.

As we consider Christ's sacrifice on the cross, we should be profoundly grateful. The Son of God wore a crown of thorns for all humanity. And He did it for you.

Christ shed His blood for you. He will walk with you through this life and throughout all eternity. So today, as you say your prayers and count your blessings, think about His sacrifice and His grace. And be thankful. Whether you're rushing through the streets of a big city or rolling through the countryside on a two-lane highway, you owe Jesus everything because He sacrificed so much for you.

God proved His love on the cross. When Christ hung, and bled, and died it was God saying to the world, "I love you."
BILLY GRAHAM

MORE FROM GOD'S WORD

Greater love has no one than this,
than to lay down one's life for his friends.
JOHN 15:13 NKJV

This is love: not that we loved God,
but that he loved us and sent his Son as
an atoning sacrifice for our sins.
1 JOHN 4:10 NIV

For when we were yet without strength,
in due time Christ died for the ungodly.
ROMANS 5:6 KJV

For God so loved the world,
that he gave his only begotten Son,
that whosoever believeth in him should not perish,
but have everlasting life.
JOHN 3:16 KJV

We love Him because He first loved us.
1 JOHN 4:19 NKJV

As Seen on Country Church Signs

When you are in deep water,
trust the One who walked on it.

Who is Jesus Christ?
Inquire within . . .

This is just a little country church
with a lost and found

Old-Time Religion

TRADITIONAL SPIRITUAL

Gimme that old-time religion.
Gimme that old-time religion.
Gimme that old-time religion.
It's good enough for me.

It was good for Paul and Silas.
It was good for Paul and Silas.
It was good for Paul and Silas.
It's good enough for me.

It was good for the Hebrew children.
It was good for the Hebrew children.
It was good for the Hebrew children.
It's good enough for me.

Makes me love ev'ry body.
Makes me love ev'ry body.
Makes me love ev'ry body.
It's good enough for me.

It Was Good for Paul and Silas

For truly I say to you, if you have faith the size of a mustard seed, you will say to this mountain, "Move from here to there," and it will move; and nothing will be impossible to you.

MATTHEW 17:20 NASB

Back in the country, old-time religion hasn't gone out of style. The simple faith that energized Paul, Silas, and countless other members of the early church is still moving mountains today. Their faith enabled them to move mountains, and you can move mountains, if you have faith.

The Bible makes it clear: faith is powerful. With faith, we can endure any hardship. With faith, we can rise above the challenges of everyday life and live victoriously, whatever our circumstances.

Is your faith strong enough to move the mountains in your own life? If so, you're already tapped in to a source of strength that never fails: God's strength. But if your spiritual batteries are in need of recharging, don't be discouraged. God's strength is always available to those who earnestly seek it. When your faith in the Creator is strong, you can have faith in yourself, knowing that you are a tool in the hands of a loving God who made mountains—and moves them—according to a perfect plan that only He can see.

I beg you to recognize the extreme simplicity of faith; it is nothing more nor less than just believing God when He says He either has done something for us, or will do it; and then trusting Him to do it. It is so simple that it is hard to explain.

HANNAH WHITALL SMITH

MORE FROM GOD'S WORD

Don't be afraid, because I am your God.
I will make you strong and will help you;
I will support you with my right hand that saves you.
ISAIAH 41:10 NCV

Don't be afraid. Only believe.
MARK 5:36 HCSB

Blessed are they that have not seen,
and yet have believed.
JOHN 20:29 KJV

All things are possible for the one who believes.
MARK 9:23 NCV

And he said unto her, Daughter,
thy faith hath made thee whole;
go in peace, and be whole.
MARK 5:34 KJV

WISDOM FROM THE FRONT PORCH

Without faith, nothing is possible.

With it, *nothing is impossible.*

-MARY MCLEOD BETHUNE

What a Friend We Have in Jesus

JOSEPH M. SCRIVEN
1855

What a friend we have in Jesus,
All our sins and griefs to bear!
What a privilege to carry
Everything to God in prayer!
O what peace we often forfeit,
O what needless pain we bear,
All because we do not carry
Everything to God in prayer!

Are we weak and heavy laden,
Cumbered with a load of care?
Precious Savior, still our refuge—
Take it to the Lord in prayer!
Do your friends despise, forsake you?
Take it to the Lord in prayer!
In his arms he'll take and shield you;
Thou wilt find a solace there.

What a Friend

As the Father loved Me, I also have loved you; abide in My love.
JOHN 15:9 NKJV

The old gospel hymn reminds us that Jesus is, quite simply, the best friend this world has ever known. Jesus loves us so much that He willingly sacrificed Himself on the cross so that we might live with Him throughout eternity. His love endures. Even when we falter, He loves us. When we fall prey to the world's temptations, He remains steadfast. In fact, no power on earth can separate us from His love.

Christ is the ultimate Savior of mankind and the personal Savior of those who believe in Him. As His servants, we should place Him at the very center of our lives, and we should share His love and His message with a world that needs both.

Jesus can transform us. When we open our hearts to Him and walk in His footsteps, our lives bear testimony to His mercy and to His grace. Yes, Christ's love changes everything. May we welcome Him into our hearts so that He can then change everything in us.

Jesus can be your friend if you let Him, when you bring Him close, when you make Him an important part of your life.
TENNESSEE ERNIE FORD

MORE FROM GOD'S WORD

I am the good shepherd. The good shepherd
lays down his life for the sheep.

JOHN 10:11 HCSB

No one has greater love than this, that someone
would lay down his life for his friends.

JOHN 15:13 HCSB

For Christ also suffered once for sins, the just for the
unjust, that He might bring us to God, being put to
death in the flesh but made alive by the Spirit.

1 PETER 3:18 NKJV

We love him, because he first loved us.

1 JOHN 4:19 KJV

For God so loved the world, that he gave his only
begotten Son, that whosoever believeth in him
should not perish, but have everlasting life.

JOHN 3:16 KJV

As Seen on Country Church Signs

History is His story.

Kneel before Jesus
and you can stand
before anyone.

Jesus.
Don't leave earth
without Him!

His Eye Is on the Sparrow

CIVILLA D. MARTIN
1905

Why should I feel discouraged? Why should the shadows come?
Why should my heart be lonely and long for heaven and home,
When Jesus is my portion? My constant friend is he:
His eye is on the sparrow, and I know he watches me;
His eye is on the sparrow, and I know he watches me.

REFRAIN:
I sing because I'm happy, (I'm happy)
I sing because I'm free, (I'm free)
For his eye is on the sparrow,
And I know he watches me.

Whenever I am tempted, whenever clouds arise,
When song gives place to sighing, when hope within me dies,
I draw the closer to him, from care he sets me free:
His eye is on the sparrow, and I know he watches me;
His eye is on the sparrow, and I know he watches me.

We Know He Watches Us

The LORD is my shepherd, I shall not want. He
makes me lie down in green pastures; He leads
me beside quiet waters. He restores my soul.

PSALM 23:1–3 NASB

God knows everything about His creation—He keeps His
watchful eye on sparrows and humans alike. Whether we're in the
heart of the big city, the far corner of the back forty, or anywhere in
between, the Creator watches over us and protects us.

The Lord is our greatest refuge. When every earthly support system fails, He remains steadfast, and His love remains
unchanged. When we encounter life's inevitable disappointments
and setbacks, the Father remains faithful. When we suffer, He is
always with us, always ready to respond to our prayers, always
working in us and through us to turn tragedy into triumph.

Thankfully, even when there's nowhere else to turn, we can
turn your thoughts and prayers to the Lord, and He will respond.
Even during life's most difficult days, God stands by us. Our job, of
course, is to return the favor and stand by Him.

Faith is not merely holding on to God.
It is God holding on to you.

CORRIE TEN BOOM

MORE FROM GOD'S WORD

The LORD is my light and my salvation—
whom should I fear? The LORD is the stronghold
of my life—of whom should I be afraid?
PSALM 27:1 HCSB

As for God, His way is perfect; the word of the Lord
is proven; He is a shield to all who trust in Him.
PSALM 18:30 NKJV

The LORD is my rock, my fortress, and my
deliverer, my God, my mountain where I seek
refuge. My shield, the horn of my salvation,
my stronghold, my refuge, and my Savior.
2 SAMUEL 22:2–3 HCSB

Those who trust in the LORD are like Mount
Zion. It cannot be shaken; it remains forever.
PSALM 125:1 HCSB

So we may boldly say: "The LORD is my helper;
I will not fear. What can man do to me?"
HEBREWS 13:6 NKJV

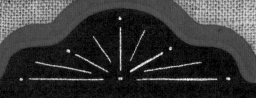

HIS EYE IS ON THE SPARROW

*T*he longer I live, the more
convincing proofs I see of this truth:

that God governs in
the affairs of man.

And if a sparrow cannot fall
to the ground without his notice,
is it probable that an empire
can rise without his aid?

BENJAMIN FRANKLIN

Overheard in an Orchard

ELIZABETH CHENEY
1859

Said the Robin to the Sparrow,
"I should really like to know
Why these anxious human beings
Rush about and worry so."

Said the Sparrow to the Robin,
"Friend, I think that it must be
That they have no Heavenly Father
Such as cares for you and me."

Why Worry?

Therefore do not worry about tomorrow, for
tomorrow will worry about its own things.
Sufficient for the day is its own trouble.
MATTHEW 6:34 NKJV

Because we are human beings who have the capacity to think and to anticipate future events, we worry. We worry about big things, little things, and just about everything in between. To make matters worse, we live in a world that breeds anxiety and fosters fear. So it's not surprising that when we come face to face with tough times, we may fall prey to discouragement, doubt, or depression. But our Father in heaven has other plans.

God has promised that we may lead lives of abundance, not anxiety. In fact, His Word instructs us to "be anxious for nothing." But how can we put our fears to rest? By taking those fears to Him and leaving them there.

The very same God who created the universe has promised to protect you now and forever. So what do you have to worry about? With God on your side, the answer is nothing.

What you trust to Him you must not worry over nor feel
anxious about. Trust and worry cannot go together.
HANNAH WHITALL SMITH

29

MORE FROM GOD'S WORD

Let not your heart be troubled;
you believe in God, believe also in Me.
JOHN 14:1 NKJV

Cast all your anxiety on him because he cares for you.
1 PETER 5:7 NIV

Peace I leave with you; My peace I give to you;
not as the world gives do I give to you. Do not
let your heart be troubled, nor let it be fearful.
JOHN 14:27 NASB

Do not be anxious about anything, but in
everything, by prayer and petition, with
thanksgiving, present your requests to God.
PHILIPPIANS 4:6 NIV

Cast your burden on the LORD, and He shall sustain
you; He shall never permit the righteous to be moved.
PSALM 55:22 NKJV

WISDOM FROM THE FRONT PORCH

Worry, like a rocking chair, will give you something to do, but it *won't get you anywhere.*

VANCE HAVNER

Swing Low, Sweet Chariot

TRADITIONAL SPIRITUAL

REFRAIN:
Swing low, sweet chariot,
Coming for to carry me home.
Swing low, sweet chariot,
Coming for to carry me home.

I looked over Jordan, and what did I see?
Coming for to carry me home.
A band of angels coming after me,
Coming for to carry me home.

If you get there before I do,
Coming for to carry me home.
Tell all my friends I'm coming too,
Coming for to carry me home.

I'm sometimes up and sometimes down,
Coming for to carry me home.
But still my soul feels heavenly bound,
Coming for to carry me home.

Heavenly Bound

Rejoice and be exceedingly glad,
for great is your reward in heaven.
MATTHEW 5:12 NKJV

Old-time country preachers spent lots of time talking about—and preaching sermons about—heaven. And with good reason. The decision to follow Christ and welcome Him into our hearts is the most important decision any of us can make.

Sometimes the troubles of this old world are easier to tolerate when we remind ourselves that heaven is our true home. This world can be a place of danger and trouble. Thankfully, the Lord has offered you a permanent home in heaven, a place of unimaginable glory, a place that your heavenly Father has already prepared for you.

Jesus has overcome the troubles of this world. We should trust Him, and we should obey His commandments. When we do, we can withstand any problem, knowing that our troubles are temporary, but that heaven is not.

If you are a Christian, you are not a citizen of this
world trying to get to heaven; you are a citizen of
heaven making your way through this world.
VANCE HAVNER

MORE FROM GOD'S WORD

For God so loved the world, that he gave his only
begotten Son, that whosoever believeth in him
should not perish, but have everlasting life.

JOHN 3:16 KJV

Most assuredly, I say to you, he who hears
My word and believes in Him who sent Me
has everlasting life, and shall not come into
judgment, but has passed from death into life.

JOHN 5:24 NKJV

Again, the kingdom of heaven is like a merchant in
search of fine pearls. When he found one priceless pearl,
he went and sold everything he had, and bought it.

MATTHEW 13:45-46 HCSB

You have this faith and love because of your hope,
and what you hope for is kept safe for you in
heaven. You learned about this hope when you heard
the message about the truth, the Good News.

COLOSSIANS 1:5 NCV

For now we see in a mirror, dimly, but then
face to face. Now I know in part, but then
I shall know just as I also am known.

1 CORINTHIANS 13:12 NKJV

As Seen on Country Church Signs

Come in and let us
prepare you
for your finals.

Visit us on your
way to eternity.

Free trip to heaven!
Details inside!

I Love to Tell The Story

KATHERINE
HANKEY
1866

I love to tell the story of unseen things above,
Of Jesus and his glory, of Jesus and his love.
I love to tell the story, because I know 'tis true;
It satisfies my longings as nothing else could do.

REFRAIN:
I love to tell the story;
'Twill be my theme in glory
To tell the old, old story
Of Jesus and his love.

I love to tell the story, for those who know it best
Seem hungering and thirsting to hear it, like the rest.
And when, in scenes of glory, I sing the new, new song,
'Twill be the old, old story that I have loved so long.

Sharing the Good News

For God has not given us a spirit of fear and timidity,
but of power, love, and self-discipline. So never
be ashamed to tell others about our Lord.
2 TIMOTHY 1:7-8 NLT

We live in a world that desperately needs the healing message of Jesus Christ. And every believer, each in his or her own way, bears a personal responsibility for sharing that message. Whether we live in the city, in the country, or anyplace in between, we all share the duty of spreading the Good News. When sharing our testimonies, we, as Christians, must be courageous, forthright, and unashamed.

If you've been transformed by God's only begotten Son, you know how He has touched your heart and changed your life. Now it's your turn to share His truth with others. And remember: now is the perfect time to share your testimony because later may quite simply be too late.

His voice leads us not into timid
discipleship but into bold witness.
CHARLES STANLEY

MORE FROM GOD'S WORD

And I say to you, anyone who acknowledges
Me before men, the Son of Man will also
acknowledge him before the angels of God.
LUKE 12:8 HCSB

You must worship Christ as Lord of your life.
And if someone asks you about your hope as
a believer, always be ready to explain it.
1 PETER 3:15 NLT

All those who stand before others and say
they believe in me, I will say before my
Father in heaven that they belong to me.
MATTHEW 10:32 NCV

When they had prayed, the place where they
were assembled was shaken, and they were
all filled with the Holy Spirit and began to
speak God's message with boldness.
ACTS 4:31 HCSB

Then He said to them, "Go into all the world
and preach the gospel to the whole creation."
MARK 16:15 HCSB

WISDOM FROM THE FRONT PORCH

If we can love folks the way they are, we have greater chance of winning them to the kingdom.

DENNIS SWANBERG

When The Roll Is Called Up Yonder

JAMES MILTON BLACK • 1893

When the trumpet of the Lord shall sound,
and time shall be no more,
And the morning breaks, eternal, bright and fair;
When the saved of earth shall gather over on the other shore,
And the roll is called up yonder, I'll be there.

REFRAIN:
When the roll is called up yonder,
When the roll is called up yonder,
When the roll is called up yonder,
When the roll is called up yonder, I'll be there.

On that bright and cloudless morning
when the dead in Christ shall rise,
And the glory of His resurrection share;
And His chosen ones shall gather
to their home beyond the skies,
And the roll is called up yonder, I'll be there.

Let us labor for the Master from the dawn till setting sun;
Let us talk of all His wondrous love and care;
Then when all of life is over, and our work on earth is done,
And the roll is called up yonder, I'll be there.

His Plan of Salvation

For God so loved the world, that he gave his only
begotten Son, that whosoever believeth in him
should not perish, but have everlasting life.

JOHN 3:16 KJV

The Son of God walked among us. He lived, loved, preached, healed, taught, and died on the cross. He did it for us. And He wants us to join Him forever in heaven.

Ours is not a distant God. He is always present, always ready to guide and protect us. He watches over His creation and He understands—far better than we ever could—the essence of what it means to be human.

God understands our fears, our hopes, and our temptations. He understands what it means to be angry and what it costs to forgive. He knows the heart and the conscience of every person who has ever lived, including you. And God has a plan of salvation that is intended for you. Accept it. Accept God's gift through the person of His Son and then rest assured: God walked among us so that you might have eternal life. Amazing though it may seem, He did it for you.

Conversion may take place in a second
of time, and so may restoration.

C. H. SPURGEON

MORE FROM GOD'S WORD

And we have seen and testify that the Father
has sent the Son as Savior of the world.
1 JOHN 4:14 NKJV

Jesus said to her, "I am the resurrection and the life.
He who believes in me will live, even though he dies;
and whoever lives by believing in me will never die."
JOHN 11:25–26 NIV

I tell you the truth,
anyone who believes has eternal life.
JOHN 6:47 NLT

Sing to the LORD, all the earth;
proclaim his salvation day after day.
1 CHRONICLES 16:23 NIV

The LORD is my strength and my song;
He has become my salvation.
EXODUS 15:2 HCSB

WISDOM FROM THE FRONT PORCH

When I first met Christ, I felt that I had *swallowed sunshine.*

E. STANLEY JONES

A Bag of Tools

R. L. SHARPE
1870–1950

Isn't it strange that princes and kings,
And clowns that caper in sawdust rings,
And common people like you and me,
Are builders for eternity?

To each is given a bag of tools,
A shapeless mass and a Book of Rules;
And each must make ere time has flown,
A stumbling block or a stepping stone.

Neighbors Helping Neighbors

The greatest among you must be a servant. But
those who exalt themselves will be humbled, and
those who humble themselves will be exalted.
MATTHEW 23:11–12 NLT

In the country, neighbors help neighbors. And that's good because God's Word instructs all of us—country folk and city folk alike—to be helpful, generous, and kind. We achieve greatness in God's eyes by serving His children gladly, humbly, and often.

Everywhere we look, the needs are great. Whether here at home or halfway around the globe, so many people are enduring difficult circumstances. They need help, and as Christians, we are instructed to serve them.

Jesus came to this world, not to conquer but to serve. We must do likewise by helping those who cannot help themselves. When we do, our lives will be blessed by the One who first served us.

The measure of a life, after all, is not
its duration but its donation.
CORRIE TEN BOOM

MORE FROM GOD'S WORD

Shepherd God's flock, for whom you are responsible.
Watch over them because you want to, not
because you are forced. That is how God wants
it. Do it because you are happy to serve.
1 PETER 5:2 NCV

As each one has received a gift, minister it to one
another, as good stewards of the manifold grace of God.
1 PETER 4:10 NKJV

Blessed are those servants, whom the lord
when he cometh shall find watching.
LUKE 12:37 KJV

Assuredly, I say to you, inasmuch as you did it to one
of the least of these My brethren, you did it to Me.
MATTHEW 25:40 NKJV

Even so faith, if it hath not works, is dead, being alone.
JAMES 2:17 KJV

As Seen on Country Church Signs

Service is just love in overalls.

Make Your Church Grow:
Some Assembly Required

Come work for the Lord.
The work is hard, the hours
are long, and the pay is low,
but the retirement benefits
are out of this world.

Standing on The Promises

RUSSELL KELSO CARTER
1886

Standing on the promises of Christ my king,
Through eternal ages let his praises ring;
Glory in the highest, I will shout and sing,
Standing on the promises of God.

REFRAIN:
Standing, standing, standing on the promises of God my Savior;
Standing, standing, I'm standing on the promises of God.

Standing on the promises that cannot fail,
When the howling storms of doubt and fear assail,
By the living Word of God I shall prevail,
Standing on the promises of God.

Standing on the promises I cannot fall,
Listening every moment to the Spirit's call,
Resting in my Savior as my all in all,
Standing on the promises of God.

Promises We Can Count On

Let us hold on to the confession of our hope without
wavering, for He who promised is faithful.
HEBREWS 10:23 HCSB

The old hymn reminds us that we can stand on the promises
that we find in God's Word. Indeed, the Bible contains promises
upon which you, as a believer, can depend. When the Creator of the
universe makes a pledge to you, He will keep it. No exceptions.

You can think of the Bible as a written contract between you
and your heavenly Father. When you fulfill your obligations to
Him, the Lord will most certainly fulfill His covenant to you.

When we accept Christ into our hearts, God promises us the
opportunity to experience contentment, peace, and spiritual abundance. But more importantly, God promises that the priceless gift
of eternal life will be ours. These promises should give us comfort.
With God on our side, we have absolutely nothing to fear in this
world and everything to hope for in the next.

From one end of the Bible to the other, God assures
us that He will never go back on His promises.
BILLY GRAHAM

MORE FROM GOD'S WORD

Sustain me as You promised, and I will live;
do not let me be ashamed of my hope.
PSALM 119:116 HCSB

As for God, his way is perfect: the word of the LORD
is tried: he is a buckler to all those that trust in him.
PSALM 18:30 KJV

They will bind themselves to the LORD with
an eternal covenant that will never be forgotten.
JEREMIAH 50:5 NLT

My God is my rock, in whom I take refuge,
my shield and the horn of my salvation.
2 SAMUEL 22:2–3 NIV

He heeded their prayer,
because they put their trust in him.
1 CHRONICLES 5:20 NKJV

There are four
words I wish we
would never forget,
and they are,

*"God
keeps His
promises."*

CHARLES SWINDOLL

Rock of Ages

AUGUSTUS MONTAGUE TOPLADY
1763

Rock of Ages, cleft for me, let me hide myself in thee;
Let the water and the blood, from thy wounded side which flowed,
Be of sin the double cure; save from wrath and make me pure.

Not the labors of my hands can fulfill thy law's demands;
Could my zeal no respite know, could my tears forever flow,
All for sin could not atone; thou must save, and thou alone.

Nothing in my hand I bring, simply to the cross I cling;
Naked, come to thee for dress; helpless, look to thee for grace;
Foul, I to the fountain fly; wash me, Savior, or I die.

While I draw this fleeting breath, when mine eyes shall close in death,
When I soar to worlds unknown, see thee on thy judgment throne,
Rock of Ages, cleft for me, let me hide myself in thee.

Standing Courageously on the Rock

The LORD is my rock and my fortress and my deliverer;
my God, my strength, in whom I will trust; my shield
and the horn of my salvation, my stronghold.
PSALM 18:2 NKJV

As believers in a risen Christ, we can, and should, live courageously. After all, Jesus promises us that He has overcome the world and that He has made a place for us in heaven. So we have nothing to fear in the long run because our Lord will care for us throughout eternity. But what about those short-term, everyday worries that keep us up at night? And what about the life-altering hardships that leave us wondering if we can ever recover? The answer, of course, is that because God cares for us in good times and hard times, we can turn our concerns over to Him in prayer, knowing that all things ultimately work for the good of those who love Him.

When you form a one-on-one relationship with your Creator, you can be comforted by the fact that wherever you find yourself, whether at the top of the mountain or the depths of the valley, God is there with you. And because your Creator cares for you and protects you, you can rise above your fears.

At this very moment the Lord is seeking to work in you and through you. He's asking you to live abundantly and courageously, and He's ready to help. So why not let Him do it...starting now?

The Rock of Ages is the great sheltering encirclement.
OSWALD CHAMBERS

MORE FROM GOD'S WORD

Be on guard. Stand firm in the faith.
Be courageous. Be strong.
1 CORINTHIANS 16:13 NLT

For God has not given us a spirit of fearfulness,
but one of power, love, and sound judgment.
2 TIMOTHY 1:7 HCSB

I can do all things through Him who strengthens me.
PHILIPPIANS 4:13 NASB

But He said to them, "It is I; do not be afraid."
JOHN 6:20 NKJV

Behold, God is my salvation; I will
trust, and not be afraid....
ISAIAH 12:2 KJV

God is in control.

He may not take away trials or make detours for us, but He strengthens us through them.

BILLY GRAHAM

Just a Closer Walk with Thee

TRADITIONAL SPIRITUAL

I am weak but Thou art strong;
Jesus, keep me from all wrong;
I'll be satisfied as long
As I walk, let me walk close to Thee.

REFRAIN:
Just a closer walk with Thee.
Grant it, Jesus, is my plea
Daily walking close to Thee,
let it be, dear Lord, let it be.

Thro' this world of toil and snares,
If I falter, Lord, who cares?
Who with me my burden shares?
None but Thee, dear Lord, none but Thee.

When my feeble life is o'er,
Time for me will be no more.
Guide me gently, safely o'er
To Thy kingdom shore, to Thy shore.

Follow Him

Then He said to them all, "If anyone
wants to come with Me, he must deny himself,
take up his cross daily, and follow Me."
LUKE 9:23 HCSB

Every day, we're presented with countless opportunities to honor God by following in the footsteps of His Son. But we're sorely tempted to do otherwise. The world is filled to the brim with temptations and distractions that beckon us down a different path.

What is your focus today? Are you willing to focus your thoughts and energies on God's blessings and upon His plan for your life? Or will you turn your thoughts to other things? Before you answer that question, consider this: the Lord created you in His own image, and He wants you to experience joy and abundance. But He will not force His joy upon you; you must claim it for yourself.

So today, do your part to take up the cross and follow Jesus, even if the world encourages you to do otherwise. When you're traveling step-by-step with the Son of God, you're always on the right path.

This is my song through endless ages:
Jesus led me all the way.
FANNY CROSBY

MORE FROM GOD'S WORD

But whoever keeps His word, truly in him the
love of God is perfected. This is how we know
we are in Him: the one who says he remains
in Him should walk just as He walked.

1 JOHN 2:5–6 HCSB

Walk in a manner worthy of the God who
calls you into His own kingdom and glory.

1 THESSALONIANS 2:12 NASB

For we walk by faith, not by sight.

2 CORINTHIANS 5:7 HCSB

Take my yoke upon you, and learn of me; for I am meek
and lowly in heart: and ye shall find rest unto your
souls. For my yoke is easy, and my burden is light.

MATTHEW 11:29–30 KJV

Whoever is not willing to carry the cross and follow
me is not worthy of me. Those who try to hold on
to their lives will give up true life. Those who give
up their lives for me will hold on to true life.

MATTHEW 10:38–39 NCV

Jesus Christ is the first and last, author and finisher, beginning and end, alpha and omega, and by Him all other things hold together. He must be first or nothing.

God never comes next!

VANCE HAVNER

Just As I Am

CHARLOTTE ELLIOTT
1835

Just as I am, without one plea,
But that thy blood was shed for me,
And that thou bidd'st me come to thee,
O Lamb of God, I come, I come.

Just as I am, and waiting not
To rid my soul of one dark blot,
To thee, whose blood can cleanse each spot,
O Lamb of God, I come, I come.

Just as I am, though tossed about
With many a conflict, many a doubt,
Fightings and fears within, without,
O Lamb of God, I come, I come.

Just as I am, thou wilt receive,
Wilt welcome, pardon, cleanse, relieve;
Because thy promise I believe,
O Lamb of God, I come, I come.

Saved by Grace

And we have known and believed the love that
God has for us. God is love, and he who abides
in love abides in God, and God in him.
1 JOHN 4:16 NKJV

God's grace is sufficient to meet our every need. No matter our circumstances, no matter our personal histories, the Lord's precious gifts are always available. All we need do is form a personal, life-altering relationship with His only begotten Son, and we're secure, now and forever.

Grace is unearned, undeserved favor from God. His grace is available to each of us. No sin is too terrible, no behavior too outrageous, to separate us from God's love. We are saved by grace through faith. Jesus paid for our sins on the cross, and when we trust Him completely, God pronounces us "not guilty" of our transgressions.

Have you accepted Christ as your King, your Shepherd, and your Savior? If so, you are protected now and forever. If not, this moment is the appropriate time to trust God's Son and accept God's grace. It's never too soon, or too late, to welcome Jesus into your heart.

How beautiful it is to learn that grace isn't fragile, and
that in the family of God we can fail and not be a failure.
GLORIA GAITHER

MORE FROM GOD'S WORD

We love him, because he first loved us.
1 JOHN 4:19 KJV

For He is gracious and compassionate,
slow to anger, rich in faithful love.
JOEL 2:13 HCSB

For God so loved the world, that he gave his only
begotten Son, that whosoever believeth in him
should not perish, but have everlasting life.
JOHN 3:16 KJV

Give thanks to Him and praise His name. For
Yahweh is good, and His love is eternal; His
faithfulness endures through all generations.
PSALM 100:4–5 HCSB

The LORD's lovingkindnesses indeed never cease,
for His compassions never fail. They are new
every morning. Great is Your faithfulness.
LAMENTATIONS 3:22–23 NASB

As Seen on Country Church Signs

If you can't sleep,
don't count sheep.
Talk to the Shepherd!

Heavenly forecast: Jesus
will REIGN forever!

Try Jesus.
If you don't like Him,
the devil will always
take you back.

Blessed Assurance

FANNY CROSBY
1873

Blessed assurance; Jesus is mine!
Oh, what a foretaste of glory divine!
Heir of salvation, purchase of God,
Born of his Spirit, washed in his blood.

REFRAIN:
This is my story, this is my song,
Praising my Savior all the day long;
This is my story, this is my song,
Praising my Savior all the day long.

Perfect submission, perfect delight,
Visions of rapture now burst on my sight;
Angels descending bring from above
Echoes of mercy, whispers of love.

Perfect submission, all is at rest,
I in my Savior am happy and blest;
Watching and waiting, looking above,
Filled with his goodness, lost in his love.

Rest Assured

Let us draw near with a true heart in full assurance
of faith, having our hearts sprinkled from an evil
conscience and our bodies washed with pure water.
HEBREWS 10:22 NKJV

No old-time hymnal would be complete without the contributions of Fanny Crosby, who was known as "the Queen of Gospel Songwriters." Despite her blindness, Crosby wrote over eight hundred songs, many of which are still sung today. One of her most popular compositions was "Blessed Assurance," a song that continues to fill the sanctuaries of little country churches, big-city churches, and mega-churches too.

Fanny Crosby understood the power of faith, and so must we. When faced with setbacks that might have embittered a lesser woman, she trusted God's promises and gratefully accepted His plan for her life.

Do you trust in the ultimate goodness of God's plan you? Will you face today's challenges with optimism and hope? You should. After all, God created you for a very important reason: His reason. And you still have important work to do: His work.

Today, as you live in the present and look to the future, remember that God is your shepherd, now and forever. When you do, you can rest assured that this day, like every other, is only a foretaste of glory divine.

Faith is the assurance that the thing which
God has said in His word is true, and that God
will act according to what He has said.
GEORGE MUELLER

MORE FROM GOD'S WORD

I will both lay me down in peace, and sleep:
for thou, LORD, only makest me dwell in safety.
PSALM 4:8 KJV

For the LORD God is a sun and shield. The LORD
gives grace and glory; He does not withhold the
good from those who live with integrity. Happy is
the person who trusts in You, LORD of Hosts!
PSALM 84:11–12 HCSB

If God be for us, who can be against us?
ROMANS 8:31 KJV

Have you not known? Have you not heard? The
everlasting God, the LORD, the Creator of the ends of
the earth, neither faints nor is weary. His understanding
is unsearchable. He gives power to the weak, and to
those who have no might He increases strength.
ISAIAH 40:28–29 NKJV

God's way is perfect. All the LORD's promises prove
true. He is a shield for all who look to him for protection.
PSALM 18:30 NLT

If you realize that there is a higher love and guidance that comes from God, then it gives you a peaceful feeling that no material possession can provide. It's the assurance, down deep, that

everything is going to be all right.

TENNESSEE ERNIE FORD

O Happy Day

PHILIP DODDRIDGE
1702–1751

O happy day that fixed my choice
On Thee, my Savior and my God!
Well may this glowing heart rejoice,
And tell its raptures all abroad.

REFRAIN:
Happy day, happy day,
When Jesus washed my sins away!
He taught me how to watch and pray,
And live rejoicing ev'ry day.
Happy day, happy day,
When Jesus washed my sins away.

'Tis done—the great transaction's done;
I am my Lord's, and He is mine;
He drew me and I followed on,
Rejoicing in the call divine.

High heav'n that hears the solemn vow,
That vow renewed shall daily hear;
Till in life's latest hour I bow,
And bless in death a bond so dear.

Where Happiness Begins

Those who listen to instruction will prosper;
those who trust the LORD will be joyful.
PROVERBS 16:20 NLT

Everywhere we turn, or so it seems, the message is clear: happiness is for sale; if we have enough money, we can buy it. But God's Word contains a different message. In the Bible, we are taught that happiness is a byproduct, the result of living in harmony with God's plan for our lives. Obedience is the path to peace, love, and happiness. Disobedience is the path to discouragement, dissatisfaction, and doubt.

Happiness also depends on the way we think. If we form the habit of focusing on the positive aspects of life, we tend to be happier. But, if we choose to dwell on the negatives, our very own thoughts have the power to make us miserable.

Do you want to be a happy Christian? Then you must start by being an obedient Christian. Whether you are sitting on the front porch of a small country home or lounging in the penthouse of the tallest building in the city, you must set your mind and heart upon God's blessings. When you count your blessings every day—and obey your Creator—you'll discover that happiness is not a commodity to be purchased; it is, instead, the natural consequence of walking daily with God.

Happy is the person who has learned to rejoice in
the simple and beautiful things around him.
BILLY GRAHAM

MORE FROM GOD'S WORD

If they obey and serve him, they will spend the rest of
their days in prosperity and their years in contentment.
JOB 36:11 NIV

I have come that they may have life,
and that they may have it more abundantly.
JOHN 10:10 NKJV

Happiness makes a person smile,
but sadness can break a person's spirit.
PROVERBS 15:13 NCV

A joyful heart is good medicine,
but a broken spirit dries up the bones.
PROVERBS 17:22 HCSB

Joyful is the person who finds wisdom,
the one who gains understanding.
PROVERBS 3:13 NLT

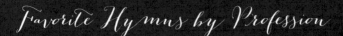

Favorite Hymns by Profession

The Realtor's Hymn: "I've Got a Mansion Just over the Hilltop"

The Gossip's Hymn: "Pass It On"

The Electrician's Hymn: "Send the Light"

The Shopper's Hymn: "In the Sweet By and By"

The Pilot's Hymn: "I'll Fly Away"

The Judge's Hymn: "Almost Persuaded"

The Baker's Hymn: "When the Roll Is Called Up Yonder"

The Shoe Repairer's Hymn: "It Is Well with My Soul"

The Librarian's Hymn: "Whispering Hope"

Onward, Christian Soldiers

SABINE BARING-GOULD
1871

Onward, Christian soldiers, marching as to war,
With the cross of Jesus going on before!
Christ, the royal Master, leads against the foe;
Forward into battle, see his banner go!

REFRAIN:
Onward, Christian soldiers, marching as to war,
With the cross of Jesus going on before!

Like a mighty army moves the church of God;
Brothers, we are treading where the saints have trod;
We are not divided; all one body we,
One in hope and doctrine, one in charity.

Onward, then, ye people, join our happy throng,
Blend with ours your voices in the triumph song;
Glory, laud, and honor, unto Christ the King;
This thro' countless ages men and angels sing.

When the Going Gets Tough

You therefore must endure hardship as
a good soldier of Jesus Christ.
2 TIMOTHY 2:3 NKJV

Tough times. Disappointments. Hardships. Pain. These experiences are the inevitable cost that each of us must pay for being human. From time to time, we all encounter adversity. Thankfully, we must never encounter it alone. God is always with us.

When we are troubled, God stands ready and willing to protect us. Our responsibility, of course, is to ask Him for protection. When we call upon Him in prayer, He will answer—in His own time and in His own way.

If you're feeling like an embattled Christian who's struggling on the battlefield of life, remember that God remains in His heaven. If you become discouraged with the direction of your day or your life, turn your thoughts and prayers to Him. He is a God of possibility, not negativity. He will guide you through your difficulties and beyond them. And then, with a renewed spirit of optimism and hope, you can thank the Giver for gifts that are simply too numerous to count.

Adversity is not simply a tool. It is God's most effective
tool for the advancement of our spiritual lives. The events
that we see as setbacks are oftentimes the very things
that launch us into periods of intense spiritual growth.
CHARLES STANLEY

MORE FROM GOD'S WORD

I called to the LORD in my distress; I called to
my God. From His temple He heard my voice.
2 SAMUEL 22:7 HCSB

The LORD is my rock, my fortress, and my
deliverer, my God, my mountain where I seek
refuge. My shield, the horn of my salvation,
my stronghold, my refuge, and my Savior.
2 SAMUEL 22:2–3 HCSB

God blesses those who patiently endure testing and
temptation. Afterward they will receive the crown of
life that God has promised to those who love him.
JAMES 1:12 NLT

He heals the brokenhearted and binds up their wounds.
PSALM 147:3 HCSB

We are hard-pressed on every side, yet not
crushed; we are perplexed, but not in despair.
2 CORINTHIANS 4:8 NKJV

As Seen on Country Church Signs

God does test us, but they are open Book tests.

Quit telling God how big your storm is and tell your storm how big your God is.

If you can't be an "Onward Christian Soldier," at least don't pass the ammunition to the enemy.

The Church in The Wildwood

WILLIAM S. PITTS
1857

There's a church in the valley by the wildwood,
No lovelier spot in the dale;
No place is so dear to my childhood
As the little brown church in the vale.

REFRAIN:
Come to the church in the wildwood,
Oh, come to the church in the vale.
No spot is so dear to my childhood
As the little brown church in the vale.

How sweet on a clear Sunday morning,
To list to the clear ringing bell;
Its tones so sweetly are calling,
Oh, come to the church in the vale.

From the church in the valley by the wildwood,
When day fades away into night,
I would fain from this spot of my childhood
Wing my way to the mansions of light.

The Little Country Church

I was glad when they said unto me,
Let us go into the house of the Lord.
PSALM 122:1 KJV

Drive down almost any country highway, and before long you'll probably spot a little country church. The typical country church serves not only as a spiritual oasis for the weary, but also as a gathering place for the entire community.

Every church, regardless of its size, needs dedicated parishioners, Christian men and women who understand the importance of sustaining—and being sustained by—their local congregations. In the book of Acts, Luke instructs us to "feed the church of God" (20:28). As Christians who have been given so much by our loving heavenly Father, we should worship Him not only in our hearts but also in the presence of fellow believers.

Today, like every other day, is a wonderful day to honor God by supporting His church. The needs are great; the laborers are few; the time for action is now; and, the blessings are real.

The church is where it's at.
The first place of Christian service
for any Christian is in a local church.
JERRY CLOWER

MORE FROM GOD'S WORD

Be on guard for yourselves and for all the flock
that the Holy Spirit has appointed you to as
overseers, to shepherd the church of God,
which He purchased with His own blood.
ACTS 20:28 HCSB

For where two or three gather
in my name, there am I with them.
MATTHEW 18:20 NIV

Enter his gates with thanksgiving, go into his courts
with praise. Give thanks to him and praise his name.
PSALM 100:4 NLT

God is Spirit, and those who worship Him
must worship in spirit and truth.
JOHN 4:24 HCSB

Worship the Lord your God, and serve Him only.
MATTHEW 4:10 HCSB

As Seen on Country Church Signs

This Church is on fire! But you don't need to call 911.

Come in and pray today—beat the Christmas rush!

If you're looking for a sign from God to get back to church, this is it!

Jesus Loves Me

ANNA BARTLETT WARNER
1860

Jesus loves me, this I know,
For the Bible tells me so.
Little ones to him belong;
They are weak, but he is strong.

REFRAIN:
Yes, Jesus loves me! Yes, Jesus loves me!
Yes, Jesus loves me! The Bible tells me so.

Jesus loves me he who died
Heaven's gate to open wide.
He will wash away my sin,
Let his little child come in.

Jesus loves me, this I know,
As he loved so long ago,
Taking children on his knee,
Saying, "Let them come to me."

Jesus Love Us, This We Know

The next day John saw Jesus coming
toward him and said, "Here is the Lamb of God,
who takes away the sin of the world!"
JOHN 1:29 HCSB

The familiar children's song reminds us of a simple, yet profound, truth: Jesus loves us. He loves us so much that He willingly sacrificed Himself on the cross so that we might live with Him throughout eternity.

Christ's love endures. Even when we falter, He loves us. When we fall prey to the world's temptations, He remains steadfast. When we make mistakes, He forgive us completely. In fact, no power on Earth can separate us from His love.

Christ's can transform us. When we open our hearts to Him and walk in His footsteps, our lives bear testimony to His mercy and His grace. Yes, Christ's love changes everything. May we welcome Him into our hearts so that He can then change everything in us.

Jesus—the standard of measurement,
the scale of weights, the test of character
for the whole moral universe.
R. G. LEE

MORE FROM GOD'S WORD

Jesus Christ the same yesterday, and to day, and for ever.
HEBREWS 13:8 KJV

I am the good shepherd. The good
shepherd gives His life for the sheep.
JOHN 10:11 NKJV

I have come as a light into the world, that whoever
believes in Me should not abide in darkness.
JOHN 12:46 NKJV

Who can separate us from the love of Christ? Can
affliction or anguish or persecution or famine or
nakedness or danger or sword?...
No, in all these things we are more than
victorious through Him who loved us.
ROMANS 8:35,37 HCSB

The thief's purpose is to steal and kill and destroy.
My purpose is to give them a rich and satisfying life.
JOHN 10:10 NLT

More Thoughts about Jesus

Look around you and you'll be distressed;
look within yourself and you'll be depressed;
look at Jesus, and you'll be at rest!
CORRIE TEN BOOM

Jesus is all compassion. He never betrays us.
CATHERINE MARSHALL

Be assured, if you walk with Him and
look to Him, and expect help from
Him, He will never fail you.
GEORGE MUELLER

The crucial question for each of us is this:
What do you think of Jesus, and do you yet
have a personal acquaintance with Him?
HANNAH WHITALL SMITH

When once you get into personal contact with
Jesus Christ, you will never be the same again.
OSWALD CHAMBERS

This Little Light of Mine

TRADITIONAL SPIRITUAL

This little light of mine, I'm gonna let it shine.
This little light of mine, I'm gonna let it shine.
This little light of mine, I'm gonna let it shine,
Let it shine, let it shine, let it shine.

Everywhere I go, I'm gonna let it shine.
Everywhere I go, I'm gonna let it shine.
Everywhere I go, I'm gonna let it shine,
Let it shine, let it shine, let it shine.

Jesus gave it to me; I'm gonna let it shine.
Jesus gave it to me; I'm gonna let it shine.
Jesus gave it to me; I'm gonna let it shine,
Let it shine, let it shine, let it shine.

Living in the Light

This is the message which we have heard
from Him and declare to you, that God is
light and in Him is no darkness at all.
1 JOHN 1:5 NKJV

God wants us to live in the light of His truth, not in the darkness of deception and despair. He wants us to live abundantly, in accordance with His teachings. And He wants us to be a worthy example to our families, to our friends, and to the world.

Every day, we make decisions that can bring us closer to God, or not. When we follow closely in the footsteps of Christ, we experience His blessings and His peace. But when we stray far from God's path, we forfeit many of the gifts that He has in store for us.

You live in a dangerous, distraction-filled world, brimming with temptations. Your task, of course, to live in the light and avoid the darkness. When you do, you'll serve as a powerful example and a positive role model in a world that surely needs both.

We must always invite Jesus to be the navigator
of our plans, desires, wills, and emotions, for
He is the way, the truth, and the life.
BILL BRIGHT

MORE FROM GOD'S WORD

I have come as a light into the world, so that everyone
who believes in Me would not remain in darkness.
JOHN 12:46 HCSB

For you were once darkness, but now you are light in
the Lord. Walk as children of light—for the fruit of
the light results in all goodness, righteousness, and
truth—discerning what is pleasing to the Lord.
EPHESIANS 5:8–10 HCSB

LORD, You are my lamp;
the LORD illuminates my darkness.
2 SAMUEL 22:29 HCSB

He who loves his brother abides in the light,
and there is no cause for stumbling in him.
1 JOHN 2:10 NKJV

You are the light that gives light to the world...
In the same way, you should be a light for other
people. Live so that they will see the good things
you do and will praise your Father in heaven.
MATTHEW 5:14, 16 NCV

Live your life so that you wouldn't be ashamed to sell the family parrot to the town gossip.

WILL ROGERS

Nearer, My God, To Thee

SARAH FLOWERS ADAMS
1805–1848

Nearer, my God, to thee, nearer to thee!
E'en though it be a cross that raiseth me,
Still all my song shall be, nearer, my God, to thee;
Nearer, my God, to thee, nearer to thee!

There let the way appear, steps unto heaven;
All that thou sendest me, in mercy given;
Angels to beckon me nearer, my God, to thee;
Nearer, my God, to thee, nearer to thee!

Then, with my waking thoughts bright with thy praise,
Out of my stony griefs Bethel I'll raise;
So by my woes to be nearer, my God, to thee;
Nearer, my God, to thee, nearer to thee!

Or if, on joyful wing cleaving the sky,
Sun, moon, and stars forgot, upward I fly,
Still all my song shall be, nearer, my God, to thee;
Nearer, my God, to thee, nearer to thee!

He's with You on the Front Porch

For the eyes of Yahweh range throughout
the earth to show Himself strong for those
whose hearts are completely His.

2 CHRONICLES 16:9 HCSB

God's love is infinite. His love spans the entirety of His creation. His love touches the far reaches of His vast universe as well as the quiet corners of every human heart.

Sometimes, amid the crush of everyday life, God may seem very far away. He is not. God is always with us, night and day. He never leaves us, even for a moment. When we earnestly seek Him, we will find Him because He is always right here, waiting patiently for us to reach out to Him. Our job, of course, is to reach out to Him.

So, whether you're in the city, the country, or anyplace else on the planet, remember that you're never alone. You're always loved and you're always protected by the Lord.

The knowledge that we are never alone
calms the troubled sea of our lives
and speaks peace to our souls.

A. W. TOZER

MORE FROM GOD'S WORD

Be still, and know that I am God.
PSALM 46:10 KJV

Draw near to God, and He will draw near to you.
JAMES 4:8 HCSB

I know the LORD is always with me.
I will not be shaken, for he is right beside me.
PSALM 16:8 NLT

Though I walk through the valley of the shadow of
death, I will fear no evil: for thou art with me.
PSALM 23:4 KJV

I am not alone, because the Father is with Me.
JOHN 16:32 NKJV

As Seen on Country Church Signs

GODISNOWHERE
(Now Read It Again)

JESUS: the Light at the
end of the tunnel.

You can believe in God now
or later. Now is better.

Shall We Gather at The River?

ROBERT LOWRY

1864

Shall we gather at the river,
Where bright angel feet have trod;
With its crystal tide forever
Flowing by the throne of God?

REFRAIN:
Yes, we'll gather at the river,
The beautiful, the beautiful river;
Gather with the saints at the river
That flows by the throne of God.

On the margin of the river,
Washing up its silver spray,
We will walk and worship ever,
All the happy golden day.

Soon we'll reach the shining river,
Soon our pilgrimage will cease;
Soon our happy hearts will quiver
With the melody of peace.

The Gift of Eternal Life

For God so loved the world,
that he gave his only begotten Son,
that whosoever believeth in him should
not perish, but have everlasting life.
JOHN 3:16 KJV

Jesus is not only the light of the world; He is also its salvation. He came to this earth so that we might not perish but instead spend eternity with Him. What a glorious gift; what a priceless opportunity.

As mere mortals, we cannot fully understand the scope, and thus the value, of eternal life. Our vision is limited, but God's is not. He sees all things; He knows all things; and His plans for you extend throughout eternity.

If you haven't already done so, this moment is the perfect moment to turn your life over to God's only begotten son. When you give your heart to the Son, you belong to the Father—today, tomorrow, and for all eternity.

When ten thousand times ten thousand
times ten thousand years have passed,
eternity will have just begun.
BILLY SUNDAY

MORE FROM GOD'S WORD

I assure you: Anyone who hears My word and believes
Him who sent Me has eternal life and will not come
under judgment, but has passed from death to life.

JOHN 5:24 HCSB

For the wages of sin is death, but the gift of
God is eternal life in Christ Jesus our Lord.

ROMANS 6:23 NIV

I have written these things to you who believe
in the name of the Son of God, so that you
may know that you have eternal life.

1 JOHN 5:13 HCSB

The world and its desires pass away, but the
man who does the will of God lives forever.

1 JOHN 2:17 NIV

The last enemy that will be destroyed is death.

1 CORINTHIANS 15:26 NKJV

As Seen on Country Church Signs

Eternity is a
long time to be wrong.

God's retirement
program for Christians
is out of this world.

If you can't stand the heat,
make plans to avoid it.

The Twenty-Third Psalm

The Lord is my shepherd; I shall not want.
He makes me to lie down in green pastures;
He leads me beside the still waters.
He restores my soul;
He leads me in the paths of righteousness
For His name's sake.

Yea, though I walk through
the valley of the shadow of death,
I will fear no evil; for You are with me;
Your rod and Your staff, they comfort me.

You prepare a table before me
in the presence of my enemies;
You anoint my head with oil; my cup runs over.
Surely goodness and mercy shall follow me
All the days of my life;
And I will dwell in the house of the Lord Forever. *NKJV*

Trust the Shepherd

When you open your Bible to its center, you'll find the book of Psalms, which contains some of the most beautiful words ever translated into the English language. Perhaps its most familiar passage, and certainly one of the most beautiful, is the twenty-third Psalm.

When David describes God as being like a shepherd, the king reminds us that the Lord constantly watches over His flock. No wonder these verses have provided comfort and hope for generations of believers.

On occasion, you will endure circumstances that break your heart and test your faith. When you are fearful, trust in God. When you are anxious, turn your worries over to Him. When you are unsure of your next step, be still and listen carefully for the Lord's guidance. And then place your life in His hands. He is your Shepherd today, tomorrow, and forever. Trust the Shepherd.

As you walk through the valley
of the unknown, you will find
the footprints of Jesus both
in front of you and beside you.
CHARLES STANLEY

MORE FROM GOD'S WORD

I will lift up mine eyes unto the hills,
from whence cometh my help.

PSALM 121:1 KJV

It is better to trust the LORD than to trust people.
It is better to trust the LORD than to trust princes.

PSALM 118:8–9 NCV

In God, whose word I praise—in God
I trust and am not afraid.

PSALM 56:4 NIV

But it is good for me to draw near to God:
I have put my trust in the LORD GOD.

PSALM 73:28 KJV

And he said: "The LORD is my rock and
my fortress and my deliverer; the God of
my strength, in whom I will trust."

2 SAMUEL 22:2–3 NKJV

MORE THOUGHTS ABOUT YOUR SHEPHERD

The Lord God of heaven and earth, the Almighty Creator,
He who holds the universe in His hand as though it
were a very little thing, He is your Shepherd, and He has
charged Himself with the care and keeping of you.
HANNAH WHITALL SMITH

Where does your security lie? Is God your refuge, your
hiding place, your stronghold, your shepherd, your counselor,
your friend, your redeemer, your savior, your guide? If He
is, you don't need to search any further for security.
ELISABETH ELLIOT

God has a course mapped out for your life, and all
the inadequacies in the world will not change His
mind. He will be with you every step of the way.
CHARLES STANLEY

God will give us the strength and resources we need to
live through any situation in life that He ordains.
BILLY GRAHAM

Since the Lord is your shepherd, what are you worried about?
MARIE T. FREEMAN

I Come To The Garden Alone

C. AUSTIN MILES
1912

I come to the garden alone,
While the dew is still on the roses;
And the voice I hear, falling on my ear,
The Son of God discloses.

REFRAIN:
And He walks with me, and He talks with me,
And He tells me I am His own,
And the joy we share as we tarry there,
None other has ever known.

He speaks, and the sound of His voice
Is so sweet the birds hush their singing;
And the melody that He gave to me
Within my heart is ringing.

I'd stay in the garden with Him
Tho' the night around me be falling;
But He bids me go; thro' the voice of woe,
His voice to me is calling.

Alone in the Garden

Now in the morning, having risen a long while
before daylight, He went out and departed to
a solitary place; and there He prayed.
MARK 1:35 NKJV

There's nothing quite like the stillness of a quiet morning spent in a country garden. When the dew is on the ground and the only things we hear are the sounds of Mother Nature, we understand that silence is, indeed, golden.

Jesus understood the importance of silence. He spent precious hours alone with God, and so should we. But with our busy schedules, we're tempted to rush from place to place, checking smart phones along the way, leaving no time to contemplate spiritual matters.

You probably live in a noisy world, a complicated society where sights and sounds surround you and silence is in short supply. Everywhere you turn, or so it seems, the media seeks to grab your attention and hijack your thoughts. You're surrounded by big screens and little ones. And your phone can keep you logged in day and night if you let it. Don't let it.

Today and every day, you need quiet, uninterrupted time alone with God. You need to be still and listen for His voice. And you need to seek His guidance in matters great and small. Your Creator has important plans for your day and your life. And He's trying to get His message through. You owe it to Him—and to yourself—to listen and to learn in silence.

The prayer offered to God in the morning during your
quiet time is the key that unlocks the door of the day.
ADRIAN ROGERS

MORE FROM GOD'S WORD

Truly my soul silently waits for God;
from Him comes my salvation.
PSALM 62:1 NKJV

Be still, and know that I am God.
PSALM 46:10 KJV

Listen in silence before me.
ISAIAH 41:1 NLT

In quietness and in confidence shall be your strength.
ISAIAH 30:15 KJV

To everything there is a season...a time to
keep silence, and a time to speak.
ECCLESIASTES 3:1,7 KJV

WISDOM FROM THE FRONT PORCH

Speed-reading may be a good thing, but it was never meant for the Bible. It takes calm, thoughtful, *prayerful meditation* on the Word to extract its deepest nourishment.

VANCE HAVNER

Sweet Hour of Prayer

W. W. WALFORD
1845

Sweet hour of prayer! sweet hour of prayer!
That calls me from a world of care,
And bids me at my Father's throne
Make all my wants and wishes known.
In seasons of distress and grief,
My soul has often found relief,
And oft escaped the tempter's snare
By thy return, sweet hour of prayer!

Sweet hour of prayer! sweet hour of prayer!
Thy wings shall my petition bear
To him whose truth and faithfulness
Engage the waiting soul to bless.
And since he bids me seek his face,
Believe his word, and trust his grace,
I'll cast on him my every care,
And wait for thee, sweet hour of prayer!

The Power of Prayer

Rejoice always, pray without ceasing,
in everything give thanks; for this is the
will of God in Christ Jesus for you.
1 THESSALONIANS 5:16-18 NKJV

No matter where you happen to be, whether you're in the city, the suburbs, the country, or anyplace in between, you always have a lifeline to God. Prayer is a powerful tool that you can use to change your world and change yourself. God hears every prayer and responds in His own way and according to His own timetable. When you make a habit of consulting Him about everything, He'll guide you along a path of His choosing, which, by the way, is the path you should take. And when you petition Him for strength, He'll give you the courage to face any problem and the power to meet any challenge.

So today, instead of turning things over in your mind, turn them over to God in prayer. Take your concerns to the Lord and leave them there. Your heavenly Father loves you; He is listening; and He wants to hear from you. Now.

I have found the perfect antidote for
fear. Whenever it sticks up its ugly
face, I clobber it with prayer.
DALE EVANS ROGERS

MORE FROM GOD'S WORD

I desire therefore that the men pray everywhere,
lifting up holy hands, without wrath and doubting.
1 TIMOTHY 2:8 NKJV

Is anyone among you suffering? He should pray.
JAMES 5:13 HCSB

Confess your trespasses to one another, and pray for
one another, that you may be healed. The effective,
fervent prayer of a righteous man avails much.
JAMES 5:16 NKJV

And whenever you stand praying, if you have anything
against anyone, forgive him, so that your Father in
heaven may also forgive you your wrongdoing.
MARK 11:25 HCSB

Ask, and it will be given to you; seek, and you
will find; knock, and it will be opened to you.
For every one who asks receives, and he who seeks
finds, and to him who knocks it will be opened.
MATTHEW 7:7–8 NASB

WISDOM FROM THE FRONT PORCH

We honor God

by asking for great
things when they are
a part of His promise.
We dishonor Him and
cheat ourselves when we
ask for molehills where He
has promised mountains.

VANCE HAVNER

Joyful, Joyful, We Adore Thee

HENRY VAN DYKE • 1907

Joyful, joyful, we adore Thee,
God of glory, Lord of love;
Hearts unfold like flow'rs before Thee,
Op'ning to the sun above.
Melt the clouds of sin and sadness;
Drive the dark of doubt away;
Giver of immortal gladness,
Fill us with the light of day!

Mortals, join the mighty chorus,
Which the morning stars began;
Father love is reigning o'er us,
Brother love binds man to man.
Ever singing, march we onward,
Victors in the midst of strife;
Joyful music leads us sunward
In the triumph song of life.

Rejoice!

This is the day which the LORD has made;
let us rejoice and be glad in it.
PSALM 118:24 NASB

The joy that the world offers is fleeting and incomplete: here today, gone tomorrow, not coming back anytime soon. But God's joy is different. His joy has staying power. In fact, it's a gift that never stops giving to those who welcome His Son into their hearts.

Psalm 100 reminds us to celebrate the lives that God has given us: "Shout for joy to the LORD, all the earth. Worship the LORD with gladness; come before him with joyful songs" (v. 1–2 NIV). Yet sometimes, amid the inevitable complications and predicaments that are woven into the fabric of everyday life, we forget to rejoice. Instead of celebrating life, we complain about it. This is an understandable mistake, but a mistake nonetheless. As Christians, we are called by our Creator to live joyfully and abundantly. To do otherwise is to squander His spiritual gifts.

This day and every day, Christ offers you His peace and His joy. Accept it and share it with others, just as He has shared His joy with you.

There is not one blade of grass,
there is no color in this world that
is not intended to make us rejoice.
JOHN CALVIN

MORE FROM GOD'S WORD

Rejoice in the Lord always. Again I will say, rejoice!
PHILIPPIANS 4:4 NKJV

Rejoice always, pray without ceasing, in everything give
thanks; for this is the will of God in Christ Jesus for you.
1 THESSALONIANS 5:16–18 NKJV

I have spoken these things to you so that My joy
may be in you and your joy may be complete.
JOHN 15:11 HCSB

Until now you have asked for nothing in My name.
Ask and you will receive, so that
your joy may be complete.
JOHN 16:24 HCSB

So you also have sorrow now. But I will
see you again. Your hearts will rejoice,
and no one will rob you of your joy.
JOHN 16:22 HCSB

Bulletin Bloopers

Next Wednesday night the church will have a potluck supper. Prayer and medication to follow.

Next Thursday there will be tryouts for the choir. They need all the help they can get.

The peacemaking meeting scheduled for Saturday has been canceled due to a conflict.

Please place your donation in the envelope along with the deceased person you want remembered.

Love Lifted Me

JAMES ROWE
1912

I was sinking deep in sin, far from the peaceful shore,
Very deeply stained within, sinking to rise no more;
But the Master of the sea heard my despairing cry,
From the waters lifted me, now safe am I.

REFRAIN:
Love lifted me! Love lifted me!
When nothing else could help,
Love lifted me.
Love lifted me! Love lifted me!
When nothing else could help,
Love lifted me.

All my heart to Him I give, ever to Him I'll cling,
In his blessed presence live, ever his praises sing.
Love so mighty and so true merits my soul's best songs;
Faithful loving service, too, to Him belongs.

Souls in danger, look above, Jesus completely saves;
He will lift you by His love out of the angry waves;
He's the master of the sea, billows His will obey;
He your Savior wants to be, be saved today.

And the Greatest of These...

And now abide faith, hope, love, these three;
but the greatest of these is love.
1 CORINTHIANS 13:13 NKJV

God is love, and He intends that we share His love with the world. But He won't force us to be loving and kind. He places that responsibility squarely on our shoulders.

Love, like everything else in this world, begins and ends with God, but the middle part belongs to us. The Creator gives each of us the opportunity to be kind, to be courteous, and to be loving. He gives each of us the chance to obey the Golden Rule, or to make up our own rules as we go. If we obey God's instructions, we're secure, but if we do otherwise, we suffer.

Christ's words are clear: "Love the Lord your God with all your heart and with all your soul and with all your mind.' This is the first and greatest commandment. And the second is like it: 'Love your neighbor as yourself.' All the Law and the Prophets hang on these two commandments" (Matthew 22:37–40 NIV). We are commanded to love the One who first loved us and then to share His love with the world. And the next move is always ours.

We need more love for the word
and less love for the world.
R. G. LEE

MORE FROM GOD'S WORD

A new commandment I give unto you,
that ye love one another; as I have loved you,
that ye also love one another.
JOHN 13:34 KJV

Love is patient, love is kind. Love does not
envy, is not boastful, is not conceited.
1 CORINTHIANS 13:4 HCSB

Beloved, if God so loved us,
we ought also to love one another.
1 JOHN 4:11 KJV

ABOVE ALL, LOVE EACH OTHER DEEPLY,
BECAUSE LOVE COVERS A MULTITUDE OF SINS. 1
PETER 4:8 NIV

And we have known and believed the love that
God has for us. God is love, and he who abides
in love abides in God, and God in him.
1 JOHN 4:16 NKJV

More Thoughts About Love

The vast ocean of Love cannot be measured
or explained, but it can be experienced.

SARAH YOUNG

The best use of life is love.
The best expression of love is time.
The best time to love is now.

RICK WARREN

You will find as you look back upon your
life that the moments when you have
truly lived are the moments when you
have done things in the spirit of love.

HENRY DRUMMOND

When we bring sunshine into the lives
of others, we're warmed by it ourselves.
When we spill a little happiness,
it splashes on us.

BARBARA JOHNSON

Softly and Tenderly Jesus Is Calling

WILL L. THOMSPON
1880

Softly and tenderly Jesus is calling,
Calling for you and for me;
See, on the portals he's waiting and watching,
Watching for you and for me.

REFRAIN:
Come home, come home;
You who are weary come home;
Earnestly, tenderly, Jesus is calling,
Calling, O sinner, come home!

Why should we tarry when Jesus is pleading,
Pleading for you and for me?
Why should we linger and heed not his mercies,
Mercies for you and for me?

O for the wonderful love he has promised,
Promised for you and for me!
Though we have sinned, he has mercy and pardon,
Pardon for you and for me.

He Renews Our Strength

Therefore, if anyone is in Christ, he is a
new creation; old things have passed away;
behold, all things have become new.
2 CORINTHIANS 5:17 NKJV

For busy citizens of the twenty-first century, it's easy to become overcommitted, overworked, over-stressed, and overwhelmed. If we choose, we can be connected 24/7, sparing just enough time to a few hours' sleep each night. What we need is time to renew and recharge, but where can we find the time? We can—and should—find it with God.

God can renew your strength and restore your spirits if you let Him. But He won't force you to slow down, and He won't insist that you get enough sleep at night. He leaves those choices up to you.

If you're feeling chronically tired or discouraged, it's time to rearrange your schedule, turn off the TV, power down the phone, and spend quiet time with your Creator. He knows what you need, and He wants you to experience His peace and His love. He's ready, willing, and perfectly able to renew your strength and help you prioritize the items on your do-list if you ask Him. In fact, He's ready to hear your prayers right now. Please don't make Him wait.

God is not running an antique shop!
He is making all things new!
VANCE HAVNER

MORE FROM GOD'S WORD

You are being renewed in the spirit of your minds;
you put on the new self, the one created according to
God's likeness in righteousness and purity of the truth.
EPHESIANS 4:23–24 HCSB

Those who hope in the LORD will renew their strength.
They will soar on wings like eagles; they will run and
not grow weary, they will walk and not be faint.
ISAIAH 40:31 NIV

Remember ye not the former things, neither consider
the things of old. Behold, I will do a new thing....
ISAIAH 43:18–19 KJV

Finally, brothers, rejoice. Be restored,
be encouraged, be of the same mind, be at peace,
and the God of love and peace will be with you.
2 CORINTHIANS 13:11 HCSB

Now the God of all grace, who called you to
His eternal glory in Christ Jesus, will personally
restore, establish, strengthen, and support you.
1 PETER 5:10 HCSB

Today is The Tomorrow we worried about yesterday.

DENNIS SWANBERG

Life's Railway To Heaven

M. E. ABBEY AND CHARLES D. TILLMAN
1890

Life is like a mountain railroad, with an engineer that's brave;
We must make the run successful, from the cradle to the grave;
Watch the curves, the fills, the tunnels; never falter, never quail;
Keep your hand upon the throttle, and your eye upon the rail.

REFRAIN:
Blessed Savior, Thou wilt guide us,
Till we reach the blissful shore,
Where the angels wait to join us
In Thy praise forevermore.

You will often find obstructions, look for storms and wind and rain;
On a fill, or curve, or trestle, they will almost ditch your train;
Put your trust alone in Jesus, never falter, never fail;
Keep your hand upon the throttle, and your eye upon the rail.

As you roll across the trestle, spanning Jordan's swelling tide,
You behold the Union Depot, into which your train will glide;
There you'll meet the Sup'rintendent, God the Father, God the Son,
With the hearty, joyous plaudit, "Weary pilgrim, welcome home."

Doing His Work

So then, each of us will give an
account of himself to God.
ROMANS 14:12 HCSB

The old saying is both familiar and true: We should pray as if everything depended upon the Lord but work as if everything depended upon us. Yet sometimes, when we are tired or discouraged, our worries can sap our strength and sidetrack our motivation. But God has other intentions. He expects us to work for the things that we pray for. More importantly, God intends that our work become His work.

As you seek to accomplish your goals and fulfill God's plan for your life, your success will depend, in large part, upon the passion that you bring to your work. God has created a world in which hard work is rewarded and laziness is not. So don't look for shortcuts (because there aren't any) and don't expect easy solutions to life's biggest challenges (because big rewards usually require lots of effort). You inhabit a world in which instant gratification is rare, but the rewards of hard work are not. Shape your expectations—and your work habits—accordingly.

It is true that we may desire much
more. But let us use what we
have, and God will give us more.
ADONIRAM JUDSON

MORE FROM GOD'S WORD

But each person should examine his own work,
and then he will have a reason for boasting in
himself alone, and not in respect to someone else.
For each person will have to carry his own load.
GALATIANS 6:4–5 HCSB

Better to be patient than powerful;
Better to have self-control than to conquer a city.
PROVERBS 16:32 NLT

Then He said to His disciples, "The harvest
is abundant, but the workers are few."
MATTHEW 9:37 HCSB

By their fruits ye shall know them.
MATTHEW 7:20 KJV

We must do the works of Him who sent Me while
it is day. Night is coming when no one can work.
JOHN 9:4 HCSB

WISDOM FROM THE FRONT PORCH

Stay busy.

Work hard.
Get proper exercise.
Eat the right foods.
Don't spend time
watching TV,
lying in bed, or
napping all day.

TRUETT CATHY

Yield Not to Temptation

DR. H. R. PALMER
1868

Yield not to temptation, for yielding is sin;
Each vict'ry will help you, some other to win;
Fight valiantly onward, evil passions subdue;
Look ever to Jesus, He will carry you through.

REFRAIN:
Ask the Savior to help you,
Comfort, strengthen and keep you;
He is willing to aid you,
He will carry you through.

Shun evil companions, bad language disdain;
God's name hold in rev'rence, nor take it in vain;
Be thoughtful and earnest, kindhearted and true;
Look ever to Jesus, He will carry you through.

To him that o'ercometh, God giveth a crown;
Through faith we will conquer, though often cast down;
He who is our Savior, our strength will renew;
Look ever to Jesus, He will carry you through.

Be Watchful

> Your adversary, the devil, prowls
> around like a roaring lion,
> seeking someone to devour.
> 1 PETER 5:8 NASB

This world can be a dangerous place: enticements are everywhere. Even if you think you're in a very safe place today, be careful. Whether you realize it or not, your adversary is near, waiting for an opening, ready to strike you down if you drop your guard. The enemy has no pity, no compassion, no remorse. And, because he's far stronger than you, he'll eventually destroy you if you try to fight him singlehandedly.

We live in a society that is brimming with temptations and distractions. Never before in the entire history of humankind have adults and children alike been offered access to so many spiritual snares. Never before has the devil had so many tools.

So beware. Take a stand against your enemy. And ask for God's protection. Because your adversary never takes a day off... and neither should you.

> A man never makes a bigger
> fool of himself than when he
> settles down in Sodom.
> VANCE HAVNER

MORE FROM GOD'S WORD

No temptation has overtaken you but such as is common
to man; and God is faithful, who will not allow you
to be tempted beyond what you are able, but with
the temptation will provide the way of escape.
1 CORINTHIANS 10:13 NASB

Do not be misled: "Bad company
corrupts good character."
1 CORINTHIANS 15:33 NIV

Put on the whole armor of God, that you may be
able to stand against the wiles of the devil.
EPHESIANS 6:11 NKJV

But encourage each other daily, while it is still called
today, so that none of you is hardened by sin's deception.
HEBREWS 3:13 HCSB

Let us lay aside every weight, and the sin
which so easily ensnares us, and let us run with
endurance the race that is set before us.
HEBREWS 12:1 NKJV

As Seen on Country Church Signs

The wages of sin
have never been reduced.

Forbidden fruits
create many jams.

All sore and weak
from backsliding? Try
pew-sitting and knee-bends.

Sweet By and By

SANFORD FILLMORE BENNETT
1868

There's a land that is fairer than day,
And by faith we can see it afar;
For the Father waits over the way
To prepare us a dwelling place there.

REFRAIN:
In the sweet by and by,
We shall meet on that beautiful shore;
In the sweet by and by,
We shall meet on that beautiful shore.

We shall sing on that beautiful shore
The melodious songs of the blest,
And our spirits shall sorrow no more,
Not a sigh for the blessing of rest.

To our bountiful Father above,
We will offer our tribute of praise
For the glorious gift of His love,
And the blessings that hallow our days.

Trust Him

Trust in the LORD with all your heart, and lean
not on your own understanding; in all your ways
acknowledge Him, and He shall direct your paths.
PROVERBS 3:5-6 NKJV

As we pass through this world, we travel past peaks and valleys. When we reach the mountaintops of life, we find it easy to praise God and to give thanks. And as we reach the crest of the mountain's peak, we find it easy to trust God's plan. But when we find ourselves in the dark valleys of life, when we face disappointment, despair, or heartbreak, it's much more difficult to trust God. Yet trust Him we must.

As Christians, we can be comforted: Whether we find ourselves at the pinnacle of the mountain or the darkest depths of the valley, God is there. And we Christians have every reason to live courageously. After all, Christ has already won the ultimate battle on the cross at Calvary.

So, the next time you find your courage tested to the limit, lean upon God's promises. Trust His Son. Remember that God is always near and that He is your protector and your deliverer. When you are worried, anxious, or afraid, call upon Him. God can handle your problems infinitely better than you can, so turn them over to Him. Remember that God rules both mountaintops and valleys—with limitless wisdom and love—now and forever.

Jesus does not say, "There is no storm."
He says, "I am here, do not toss, but trust."
VANCE HAVNER

MORE FROM GOD'S WORD

In quietness and trust is your strength.
ISAIAH 30:15 NASB

The LORD is my rock, my fortress, and my
deliverer, my God, my mountain where I seek
refuge. My shield, the horn of my salvation,
my stronghold, my refuge, and my Savior.
2 SAMUEL 22:2-3 HCSB

The fear of man is a snare, but the one
who trusts in the LORD is protected.
PROVERBS 29:25 HCSB

Those who trust in the LORD are like Mount
Zion. It cannot be shaken; it remains forever.
PSALM 125:1 HCSB

Jesus said, "Don't let your hearts be troubled.
Trust in God, and trust in me."
JOHN 14:1 NCV

WISDOM FROM THE FRONT PORCH

Never imagine
that you can
be a loser by
*Trusting
in God.*

C. H. SPURGEON

Bringing In The Sheaves

KNOWLES SHAW
1874

Sowing in the morning, sowing seeds of kindness,
Sowing in the noontide and the dewy eve;
Waiting for the harvest, and the time of reaping,
We shall come rejoicing, bringing in the sheaves.

REFRAIN:
Bringing in the sheaves, bringing in the sheaves,
We shall come rejoicing, bringing in the sheaves;
Bringing in the sheaves, bringing in the sheaves,
We shall come rejoicing, bringing in the sheaves.

Sowing in the sunshine, sowing in the shadows,
Fearing neither clouds nor winter's chilling breeze;
By and by the harvest, and the labor ended,
We shall come rejoicing, bringing in the sheaves.

Going forth with weeping, sowing for the Master,
Tho' the loss sustained our spirit often grieves;
When our weeping's over, He will bid us welcome,
We shall come rejoicing, bringing in the sheaves.

Celebrate Every Day

Rejoice in the Lord always.
Again I will say, rejoice!
PHILIPPIANS 4:4 NKJV

Because each day is a gift from God, it's a cause for celebration. And each day has its own share of blessings. Our assignment, as grateful believers, is to look for the blessings and celebrate them.

Country singer Reba McEntire begins each day with a prayer. She raises her arms and says, "Thank You, Lord Jesus, Father God, and Holy Spirit. Thank You for a wonderful night's sleep. This is going to be a wonderful day because You made it." We all should have similar sentiments.

Today, like every other, is a priceless gift from the Creator. He has offered us yet another opportunity to serve Him with smiling faces and willing hands. When we do our part, He inevitably does His part, and miracles happen.

The Lord has promised to bless you and keep you, now and forever. So, don't wait for birthdays or holidays. Make this day an exciting adventure. And while you're at it, take time to thank God for His blessings. He deserves your gratitude, and you deserve the joy of expressing it.

Every day we live is a priceless gift of God, loaded with possibilities to learn something new, to gain fresh insights.
DALE EVANS ROGERS

133

MORE FROM GOD'S WORD

A happy heart is like a continual feast.
PROVERBS 15:15 NCV

This is the day which the LORD has made;
let us rejoice and be glad in it.
PSALM 118:24 NASB

Rejoice always, pray without ceasing, in
everything give thanks; for this is the
will of God in Christ Jesus for you.
1 THESSALONIANS 5:16–18 NKJV

I delight greatly in the LORD;
my soul rejoices in my God.
ISAIAH 61:10 NIV

I came that they may have life,
and have it abundantly.
JOHN 10:10 NASB

Favorite Hymns by Profession

The Contractor's Hymn:
"The Church's One Foundation"

The Dentist's Hymn:
"Crown Him with Many Crowns"

The Weatherman's Hymn:
"There Shall Be Showers of Blessing"

The Tailor's Hymn: "Holy, Holy, Holy"

The Golfer's Hymn:
"There Is A Green Hill Far Away"

The Politician's Hymn:
"Standing on the Promises"

The Optometrist's Hymn:
"Open My Eyes That I May See"

Lord, I Want to Be a Christian

TRADITIONAL SPIRITUAL

Lord, I want to be a Christian in my heart, in my heart.
Lord, I want to be a Christian in my heart.
In my heart, in my heart,
Lord, I want to be a Christian in my heart.

Lord, I want to be more loving in my heart, in my heart.
Lord, I want to be more loving in my heart.
In my heart, in my heart,
Lord, I want to be more loving in my heart.

Lord, I want to be more holy in my heart, in my heart.
Lord, I want to be more holy in my heart.
In my heart, in my heart,
Lord, I want to be more holy in my heart.

Lord, I want to be like Jesus in my heart, in my heart.
Lord, I want to be like Jesus in my heart.
In my heart, in my heart,
Lord, I want to be like Jesus in my heart.

The Righteous Life

Live peaceful and quiet lives
in all godliness and holiness.
1 TIMOTHY 2:2 NIV

Every life, including yours, is a series of choices. Each day, you make countless decisions that will bring you closer to God, or not. The Lord wants you to live a holy life, a life that reflects an understanding of His Word and a love for His Son.

If we seek God's peace and His blessings, we must respect His teachings and obey them. When we're faced with a difficult choice or a powerful temptation, we should seek God's counsel and trust the counsel He gives.

The Holy Bible contains careful instructions that, if followed, lead to fulfillment and salvation. But if we choose to ignore God's commandments, the results are as predictable as they are tragic. So if you'd like a simple, surefire formula for abundant living, here it is: live righteously. And for further instructions, read the manual.

Holiness, not happiness,
is the chief end of man.
OSWALD CHAMBERS

MORE FROM GOD'S WORD

The pure in heart are blessed,
for they will see God.
MATTHEW 5:8 HCSB

But seek first the kingdom of God
and His righteousness, and all these
things shall be added to you.
MATTHEW 6:33 NKJV

The highway of the upright avoids evil;
the one who guards his way protects his life.
PROVERBS 16:17 HCSB

He who follows righteousness and mercy
finds life, righteousness and honor.
PROVERBS 21:21 NKJV

For the LORD knows the way of the righteous,
but the way of the ungodly shall perish.
PSALM 1:6 NKJV

WISDOM FROM THE FRONT PORCH

The messages from hymns
and feelings that come from
them are an important
part of living. They help
make a sad man happy
and a happy man happier,
a bad man good and

*a good man
better.*

TENNESSEE ERNIE FORD

Revive Us Again

WILLIAM P. MACKAY
1863

We praise Thee, O God!
For the Son of Thy love,
For Jesus who died,
And is now gone above.

REFRAIN:
Hallelujah! Thine the glory.
Hallelujah! Amen.
Hallelujah! Thine the glory.
Revive us again.

We praise Thee, O God!
For Thy Spirit of light,
Who hath shown us our Savior,
And scattered our night.

All glory and praise
to the Lamb that was slain,
who hath borne all our sins,
and hath cleansed every stain.

The Old-Time Revival

I preached that they should repent
and turn to God and demonstrate
their repentance by their deeds.
ACTS 26:20 NIV

Revival meetings still provide important opportunities to inspire church members and recruit new converts. Historically, revivals have been particularly important to small country churches. The meetings often result in conversions, rededications, and a renewed sense of energy in the church.

As Christians, we are called to share the Good News of Jesus Christ with our families, with our neighbors, and with the world. Jesus commanded His disciples to become fishers of men. We must do likewise.

Revivals have an important place in the lives of many churches, and a revival can play an important role in your life, too. So, the next time your church hosts an old-fashioned revival meeting, be an enthusiastic participant. And remember that every revival meeting provides yet another opportunity for someone in your community to find Christ.

Be filled with the Holy Spirit; join a church where the
members believe the Bible and know the Lord; seek the
fellowship of other Christians; learn and be nourished
by God's Word and His many promises. Conversion is
not the end of your journey—it is only the beginning.
CORRIE TEN BOOM

MORE FROM GOD'S WORD

For everyone who calls on the name
of the Lord will be saved.

ROMANS 10:13 HCSB

You have been born again, and this new life did not
come from something that dies, but from something
that cannot die. You were born again through
God's living message that continues forever.

1 PETER 1:23 NCV

When we were baptized, we were buried with
Christ and shared his death. So, just as Christ
was raised from the dead by the wonderful power
of the Father, we also can live a new life.

ROMANS 6:4 NCV

That which is born of the flesh is flesh; and
that which is born of the Spirit is spirit.

JOHN 3:6 KJV

Therefore, if anyone is in Christ, he is
a new creation; old things have passed
away, and look, new things have come.

2 CORINTHIANS 5:17 HCSB

Evangelism is the proclamation of the gospel with the purpose of *winning the lost to Christ.*

Revival is a fresh work of the Holy Spirit among Christians to bring them to confession of sin, renewed dedication, and loving zeal for service.

VANCE HAVNER

All Hail The Power of Jesus' Name

EDWARD PERRONET • 1780

All hail the power of Jesus' name!
Let angels prostrate fall.
Bring forth the royal diadem,
and crown him Lord of all.
Bring forth the royal diadem,
and crown him Lord of all!

Ye chosen seed of Israel's race
Ye ransomed from the fall,
hail him who saves you by his grace,
and crown him Lord of all.
Hail him who saves you by his grace,
and crown him Lord of all!

Let every tongue and every tribe
On this terrestrial ball,
To him all majesty ascribe,
and crown him Lord of all.
To him all majesty ascribe,
and crown him Lord of all!

Praise Him

Let everything that breathes
praise the Lord. Hallelujah!
PSALM 150:6 HCSB

The Bible teaches us to praise God, but sometimes we become so preoccupied with the challenges and demands of everyday life that we forget to say thank you to the Giver of all good gifts.

Praise and worship should never be relegated to Sunday mornings; instead, we should weave prayer and thanksgiving into every aspect of everyday life.

Theologian Wayne Oates once admitted, "Many of my prayers are made with my eyes open. You see, it seems I'm always praying about something, and it's not always convenient—or safe—to close my eyes." Dr. Oates understood that God always hears our prayers and that the relative position of our eyelids is of no concern to Him.

If you sincerely desire to be a worthy servant of the One who has given you eternal love and eternal life, praise Him for who He is and for what He has done for you. Don't just praise Him on Sunday. Praise Him throughout the day, every day, for as long as you live...and then for all eternity.

The best moment to praise God
is always the present one.
MARIE T. FREEMAN

MORE FROM GOD'S WORD

Great is the Lord! He is most worthy of praise!
No one can measure his greatness.
PSALM 145:3 NLT

In everything give thanks; for this is
the will of God in Christ Jesus for you.
1 THESSALONIANS 5:18 NKJV

At the name of Jesus every knee should bow,
of things in heaven, and things in earth,
and things under the earth; and that every
tongue should confess that Jesus Christ
is Lord, to the glory of God the Father.
PHILIPPIANS 2:10-11 KJV

The LORD is my strength and my song;
He has become my salvation.
EXODUS 15:2 HCSB

From the rising of the sun to its setting,
the name of the LORD is to be praised.
PSALM 113:3 NASB

I can still close my eyes
and see those Sundays
in the little church
we filled up with praise.
I can still hear those

*lovely voices
lifted up
to God.*

REBA MCENTIRE

Whispering Hope

SEPTIMUS WINNER
1868

Soft as the voice of an angel, breathing a lesson unheard,
Hope with a gentle persuasion whispers her comforting word:
Wait till the darkness is over, wait till the tempest is done,
Hope for the sunshine tomorrow, after the shower is gone.

REFRAIN:
Whispering hope, oh, how welcome thy voice,
Making my heart in its sorrow rejoice.

If, in the dusk of the twilight, dim be the region afar,
Will not the deepening darkness brighten the glimmering star?
Then when the night is upon us, why should the heart sink away?
When the dark midnight is over, watch for the breaking of day.

Hope, as an anchor so steadfast, rends the dark veil for the soul,
Whither the Master has entered, robbing the grave of its goal;
Come then, oh, come, glad fruition, come to my sad weary heart;
Come, O Thou blest hope of glory, never, oh, never depart.

Be Hopeful

Let us hold fast the confession
of our hope without wavering,
for He who promised is faithful.
HEBREWS 10:23 NASB

God's promises give us hope: hope for today, hope for tomorrow, hope for all eternity. The hope that the world offers is temporary, at best. But the hope that God offers never grows old and never goes out of date. It's no wonder, then, that when we pin our hopes on worldly resources, we are often disappointed. Thankfully, God has no such record of failure.

The Bible teaches that the Lord blesses those who trust in His wisdom and follow in the footsteps of His Son. Will you count yourself among that number? When you do, you'll have every reason on earth—and in heaven—to be hopeful about your future. After all, God has made important promises to you, promises that He is certainly going to keep. So be hopeful, be optimistic, be faithful, and do your best. Then, leave the rest up to God. Your destiny is safe with Him.

Darkness may throw a shadow over my outer
vision, but there is no cloud that can keep the
sunlight of hope from a trustful soul.
FANNY CROSBY

MORE FROM GOD'S WORD

This hope we have as an anchor
of the soul, a hope both sure and steadfast.
HEBREWS 6:19 NASB

I say to myself, "The LORD
is mine, so I hope in him."
LAMENTATIONS 3:24 NCV

The LORD is good to those who wait
for Him, to the soul who seeks Him.
It is good that one should hope and wait
quietly for the salvation of the LORD.
LAMENTATIONS 3:25–26 NKJV

Hope deferred makes the heart sick.
PROVERBS 13:12 NKJV

Be strong and courageous,
all you who put your hope in the LORD.
PSALM 31:24 HCSB

More Thoughts about Hope

We carry a bag of spending money in our hands, but the bulk of our wealth is deposited in the Bank of Hope.

C. H. SPURGEON

God is the only one who can make the valley of trouble a door of hope.

CATHERINE MARSHALL

Come up from the lowlands; there are heights yet to climb. You cannot do healthful thinking in the lowlands. Look to the mountaintop for faith.

MARY MCLEOD BETHUNE

Two types of voices command your attention today. Negative ones fill your mind with doubt, bitterness, and fear. Positive ones purvey hope and strength. Which one will you choose to heed?

MAX LUCADO

If your hopes are being disappointed just now, it means that they are being purified.

OSWALD CHAMBERS

I Need Thee Every Hour

ANNIE S. HAWKS AND
ROBERT LOWRY
1872

I need thee every hour, most gracious Lord;
No tender voice like thine can peace afford.

REFRAIN:
I need thee, O I need thee, every hour I need thee.
O bless me now, my Savior; I come to thee.

I need thee every hour; stay thou nearby;
Temptations lose their power when thou art nigh.

I need thee every hour, Most Holy One;
O make me thine indeed, thou Blessed Son!

Experiencing His Peace

Peace I leave with you, My peace I give to you;
not as the world gives do I give to you. Let not
your heart be troubled, neither let it be afraid.

JOHN 14:27 NKJV

Peace is such a lovely word. It conveys images of tranquility, contentment, serenity, and freedom from the trials and tribulations of everyday life. Peace means freedom from outer struggles and inner turmoil. Peace is such a beautiful concept that advertisers and marketers attempt to sell it with images of relaxed vacationers lounging on the beach or happy senior citizens celebrating on the golf course. But contrary to the implied claims of modern media, real peace, genuine, lasting peace isn't for sale. At any price.

Have you discovered the genuine peace that can be yours through Christ? Or are you still pursuing the illusion of peace that the world promises but cannot deliver? If you've turned things over to Jesus, you'll be blessed. And you'll experience the only peace that really matters: God's peace.

Jesus did not promise to change the circumstances
around us. He promised great peace and
pure joy to those who would learn to believe
that God actually controls all things.

CORRIE TEN BOOM

MORE FROM GOD'S WORD

He Himself is our peace.
EPHESIANS 2:14 NASB

The peace of God, which passeth all
understanding, shall keep your hearts
and minds through Christ Jesus.
PHILIPPIANS 4:7 KJV

But the fruit of the Spirit is love, joy, peace,
patience, kindness, goodness, faith, gentleness,
self-control. Against such things there is no law.
GALATIANS 5:22–23 HCSB

"I will give peace, real peace, to those far and
near, and I will heal them," says the LORD.
ISAIAH 57:19 NCV

These things I have spoken to you,
that in Me you may have peace. In the
world you will have tribulation; but be
of good cheer, I have overcome the world.
JOHN 16:33 NKJV

As Seen on Country Church Signs

No Jesus, no peace.
Know Jesus, know peace!

Trade God your pieces
for His peace.

Some hearts need a
pace-maker; all hearts
need the Peace-maker.

Count Your Blessings

JOHN OATMAN, JR.
1897

When upon life's billows you are tempest tossed,
When you are discouraged, thinking all is lost,
Count your many blessings, name them one by one,
And it will surprise you what the Lord hath done.

REFRAIN:
Count your blessings, name them one by one;
Count your blessings, see what God hath done;
Count your blessings, name them one by one;
Count your many blessings, see what God hath done.

Are you ever burdened with a load of care?
Does the cross seem heavy you are called to bear?
Count your many blessings, ev'ry doubt will fly,
And you will be singing as the days go by.

So, amid the conflict, whether great or small,
Do not be discouraged, God is over all;
Count your many blessings, angels will attend,
Help and comfort give you to your journey's end.

Truly Blessed

Yahweh bless you and protect you;
Yahweh make His face shine on
you, and be gracious to you.
NUMBERS 6:24-25 HCSB

If you settled into a rocking chair on your front porch and began counting all your blessings, how long would it take? The answer, of course, is a very, very long time. After all, you've been given the priceless gift of life here on earth and the promise of life eternal in heaven. And you've been given so much more.

Billy Graham noted: "We should think of the blessings we so easily take for granted: life itself; preservation from danger; every bit of health we enjoy; every hour of liberty; the ability to see, to hear, to speak, to think, and to imagine all this comes from the hand of God." That's sound advice for believers—followers of the One from Galilee—who have so much to be thankful for.

Your blessings, all of which are gifts from above, are indeed too numerous to count, but it never hurts to begin counting them anyway. It never hurts to say thanks to the Giver for the gifts you can count, and all the other ones, too.

God is the giver, and we are the receivers.
And His richest gifts are bestowed not upon
those who do the greatest things, but upon those
who accept His abundance and His grace.
HANNAH WHITALL SMITH

MORE FROM GOD'S WORD

You will show me the path of life;
in Your presence is fullness of joy;
at Your right hand are
pleasures forevermore.
PSALM 16:11 NKJV

The LORD is good to all:
and his tender mercies are over all his works.
PSALM 145:9 KJV

The LORD is my rock, my fortress, and my
deliverer, my God, my mountain where I seek
refuge. My shield, the horn of my salvation,
my stronghold, my refuge, and my Savior.
2 SAMUEL 22:2–3 HCSB

The LORD is my shepherd; I shall not want.
PSALM 23:1 KJV

Blessings crown the head of the righteous....
PROVERBS 10:6 NIV

As Seen on Country Church Signs

When you harbor bitterness, happiness will dock elsewhere.

Get rich quick! Count your blessings!

Count your blessings. Recounts are OK!

Jesus, Savior, Pilot Me

EDWARD HOPPER
1871

Jesus, Savior, pilot me
Over life's tempestuous sea;
Unknown waves before me roll,
Hiding rock and treach'rous shoal.
Chart and compass come from Thee.
Jesus, Savior, pilot me.

As a mother stills her child,
Thou canst hush the ocean wild;
Boist'rous waves obey Thy will
When Thou sayest to them, "Be still!"
Wondrous Sovereign of the sea,
Jesus, Savior, pilot me.

When at last I near the shore,
And the fearful breakers roar
'Twixt me and the peaceful rest,
Then, while leaning on Thy breast,
May I hear Thee say to me,
"Fear not, I will pilot thee."

Trust His Guidance

Trust in the LORD with all your heart, and lean
not on your own understanding; in all your ways
acknowledge Him, and He shall direct your paths.

PROVERBS 3:5-6 NKJV

When we ask for God's guidance, with our hearts and minds open to His direction, He will lead us along a path of His choosing. But for many of us, listening to God is hard. We have so many things we want, and so many needs to pray for, that we spend far more time talking at God than we do listening to Him.

Every day that we awaken, we are confronted with countless opportunities to serve God and to worship Him. When we do, He blesses us. But when we turn our backs to the Creator, or when we are simply too busy to acknowledge His greatness, we do a profound disservice to ourselves, to our families, and to the world. Things always go best when we seek the Lord's direction early and often. Our Father has many ways to make Himself known. Our challenge is to make ourselves open to His instruction.

So, if you're unsure of your next step, trust God's promises and talk to Him often. When you do, He'll guide your steps today, tomorrow, and forever.

God's guidance is even more important than
common sense. I can declare that the deepest
darkness is outshone by the light of Jesus.

CORRIE TEN BOOM

MORE FROM GOD'S WORD

Yet LORD, You are our Father;
we are the clay, and You are our potter;
we all are the work of Your hands.

ISAIAH 64:8 HCSB

The LORD says, "I will guide you along
the best pathway for your life. I will
advise you and watch over you."

PSALM 32:8 NLT

Teach me to do Your will, for You are my God;
Your Spirit is good. Lead me in the land of uprightness.

PSALM 143:10 NKJV

Shew me thy ways, O LORD; teach me thy paths.
Lead me in thy truth, and teach me: for thou art the
God of my salvation; on thee do I wait all the day.

PSALM 25:4–5 KJV

Morning by morning he wakens me and opens
my understanding to his will. The Sovereign
Lord has spoken to me, and I have listened.

ISAIAH 50:4–5 NLT

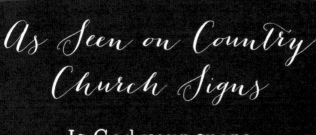

As Seen on Country Church Signs

Is God your spare wheel or your steering wheel?

God answers knee-mail.

If God is your co-pilot, swap seats!

Hold to God's Unchanging Hand

JENNIE B. WILSON
1906

Time is filled with swift transition,
Naught of earth unmoved can stand,
Build your hopes on things eternal,
Hold to God's unchanging hand.

REFRAIN:
Hold to God's unchanging hand,
Hold to God's unchanging hand;
Build your hopes on things eternal,
Hold to God's unchanging hand.

Trust in Him who will not leave you,
Whatsoever years may bring,
If by earthly friends forsaken
Still more closely to Him cling.

When your journey is completed,
If to God you have been true,
Fair and bright the home in glory
Your enraptured soul will view.

Our Circumstances Change But God Doesn't

To every thing there is a season,
and a time to every purpose under the heaven.
ECCLESIASTES 3:1 KJV

Even in sleepy small towns, things change. People change; surroundings change; technologies change; even habits change. It's simply a fact of life: the world keeps changing and so do we. Thankfully, God doesn't change. And neither do His promises.

God's Word makes it clear: "I am the LORD, I do not change" (Malachi 3:6 NKJV). So we can be comforted by the knowledge that our covenant with the Creator is everlasting and nonnegotiable. The Lord has promised to keep His word, and that's precisely what He will do.

The next time you face tough times or unwelcome changes, remember that one thing never changes: God's love for you. Then, perhaps, you'll worry less, do your best, and leave the rest up to Him.

The world changes—circumstances change,
we change—but God's Word never changes.
WARREN WIERSBE

MORE FROM GOD'S WORD

The wise see danger ahead and avoid it,
but fools keep going and get into trouble.
PROVERBS 22:3 NCV

But grow in the grace and knowledge of our
Lord and Savior Jesus Christ. To Him be the
glory both now and forever. Amen.
2 PETER 3:18 NKJV

When I was a child, I spoke like a child,
I thought like a child, I reasoned like a child.
When I became a man, I put aside childish things.
1 CORINTHIANS 13:11 HCSB

Then He who sat on the throne said,
"Behold, I make all things new."
REVELATION 21:5 NKJV

God, create a clean heart for me and
renew a steadfast spirit within me.
PSALM 51:10 HCSB

When all else
is gone,
*God is
still left.*
Nothing
changes Him.

HANNAH WHITALL SMITH

The House by the Side of the Road

SAM WALTER FOSS
1858–1911

There are hermit souls that live withdrawn
In the place of their self-content;
There are souls like stars, that dwell apart,
In a fellowless firmament;
There are pioneer souls that blaze their paths
Where highways never ran—
But let me live by the side of the road
And be a friend to man.

Let me live in my house by the side of the road—
It's here the race of men go by.
They are good, they are bad, they are weak, they are strong,
Wise, foolish—so am I;
Then why should I sit in the scorner's seat,
Or hurl the cynic's ban?
Let me live in my house by the side of the road
And be a friend to man.

The Gift of Encouragement

But encourage each other daily,
while it is still called today, so that none
of you is hardened by sin's deception.
HEBREWS 3:13 HCSB

Whether we realize it or not, all of us need encouragement. The world can be a difficult place, a place where we encounter the inevitable disappointments that are woven into the fabric of everyday life. So we all need boosters who are ready, willing, and able to cheer us on when times get tough.

God's Word teaches that we must treat others as we ourselves wish to be treated. Since we desire encouragement for ourselves, we should be quick to share it with others.

Whom will you encourage today? How many times will you share a smile, or a kind word, or a pat on the back? You'll probably have many opportunities to share the gift of encouragement. When you seize those opportunities, others will be blessed, and you'll be blessed, too. But not necessarily in that order.

Discouraged people don't need critics. They hurt
enough already. They don't need more guilt or
piled-on distress. They need encouragement. They need
a refuge, a willing, caring, available someone.
CHARLES SWINDOLL

MORE FROM GOD'S WORD

Let us think about each other and help each
other to show love and do good deeds.
HEBREWS 10:24 ICB

Bear one another's burdens,
and so fulfill the law of Christ.
GALATIANS 6:2 NKJV

So encourage each other and give each other
strength, just as you are doing now.
1 THESSALONIANS 5:11 NCV

When you talk, do not say harmful things,
but say what people need—words that will help
others become stronger. Then what you say
will do good to those who listen to you.
EPHESIANS 4:29 NCV

Now we exhort you, brethren, warn those
who are unruly, comfort the fainthearted,
uphold the weak, be patient with all.
1 THESSALONIANS 5:14 NKJV

Old-Time Hymns

REVISED FOR POLITICAL CORRECTNESS
AND MODERN SENSIBILITIES

"Amazing Grace, How Interesting the Sound"

"Pillow of Ages, Fluffed for Me"

"What an Acquaintance We Have in Jesus"

"Blessed Insurance"

"I Surrender Some"

"Onward, Christian Social Workers"

"Standing on the Premises"

"Sweet Minute of Prayer"

And the All-Time Children's Classic:
"I Love Me, This I Know"

The Touch of the Master's Hand

MYRA BROOKS WELCH
1921

'Twas battered and scarred,
And the auctioneer thought it hardly worth his while
To waste his time on the old violin,
but he held it up with a smile.

"What am I bid, good people," he cried,
"Who starts the bidding for me?"
"One dollar, one dollar, do I hear two?"
"Two dollars, who makes it three?"

"Three dollars once, three dollars twice, going for three."

But, no,
From the room far back a gray bearded man
Came forward and picked up the bow.
Then wiping the dust from the old violin
And tightening up the strings,
He played a melody, pure and sweet,
As sweet as the angel sings.

The music ceased and the auctioneer
With a voice that was quiet and low,
Said "What now am I bid for this old violin?"
As he held it aloft with its bow.

"One thousand, one thousand, do I hear two?"
"Two thousand, who makes it three?"
"Three thousand once, three thousand twice,
Going and gone," said he.

The audience cheered, but some of them cried,
"We just don't understand."
"What changed its worth?" Swift came the reply.
"The Touch of the Master's Hand."

And many a man with life out of tune
All battered and bruised with hardship
Is auctioned cheap to a thoughtless crowd
Much like that old violin

A mess of pottage, a glass of wine,
A game and he travels on.
He is going once, he is going twice,
He is going and almost gone.

But the Master comes,
And the foolish crowd never can quite understand,
The worth of a soul and the change that is wrought
By the Touch of the Master's Hand.

Using Your Talents

Do not neglect the gift that is in you.
1 TIMOTHY 4:14 NKJV

God gives each of us special talents and opportunities. And He bestows these gifts for a reason: so that we might use them for His glory. But the world tempts us to do otherwise. Here in the twenty-first century, life is filled to the brim with distractions and temptations, each of which has the potential to distance us from the path God intends for us to take.

Do you possess financial resources? Share them. Do you have a spiritual gift? Share it. Do you have a personal testimony about the things that Christ has done for you? Tell your story. Do you possess a particular talent? Hone that skill and use it for God's glory.

All your talents, all your opportunities, and all your gifts are on temporary loan from the Creator. Use those gifts while you can because time is short and the needs are great. In every undertaking, make God your partner. Then, just as He promised, God will bless you now and forever.

God has given you special talents—
now it's your turn to give them back to God.
MARIE T. FREEMAN

MORE FROM GOD'S WORD

God has given each of you a gift
from his great variety of spiritual gifts.
Use them well to serve one another.
1 PETER 4:10 NLT

Now there are diversities of gifts, but the same Spirit.
1 CORINTHIANS 12:4 KJV

Every good and perfect gift is from above,
coming down from the Father of the heavenly lights,
who does not change like shifting shadows.
JAMES 1:17 NIV

His master replied, "Well done, good and faithful servant! You
have been faithful with a few things; I will put you in charge
of many things. Come and share your master's happiness!"
MATTHEW 25:21 NIV

I remind you to fan into flame the gift of God.
2 TIMOTHY 1:6 NIV

Home, Sweet Home

JOHN HOWARD PAYNE
1791–1852

'Mid pleasures and palaces tho' we may roam,
Be it ever so humble, there's no place like home.
A charm from the skies seems to hallow us there,
Which, seek thro' the world, is ne'er met with elsewhere.

Home, home, sweet, sweet home,
Be it ever so humble, there's no place like home.

An exile from home, splendor dazzles in vain;
Oh, give me my lowly thatched cottage again.
The birds singing gaily, that came at my call;
Oh, give me that peace of mind, dearer than all.

Home, home, sweet, sweet home,
Be it ever so humble, there's no place like home.

There's No Place Like Home

Choose for yourselves today the one
you will worship....As for me and
my family, we will worship Yahweh.
JOSHUA 24:15 HCSB

A happy home is a treasure from God. If the Lord has blessed you with a close-knit family and a peaceful home, give thanks to your Creator because He has given you one of His most precious earthly possessions.

You inhabit a demanding world, a place where life can be tough and pressures can be intense. Even when the demands of everyday life are great, you must never forget that you have been entrusted with a profound responsibility: the responsibility of contributing to your family's emotional and spiritual health. It's a big job, but with the Lord's help, you can do it.

So the next time your home life becomes stressful, remember that your loved ones are a gift from above. You should praise God for that gift—and you should act accordingly.

The mind of Christ is to be learned in the family.
Strength of character may be acquired at work,
but beauty of character is learned at home.
HENRY DRUMMOND

MORE FROM GOD'S WORD

Unless the LORD builds a house,
its builders labor over it in vain;
unless the LORD watches over a city,
the watchman stays alert in vain.
PSALM 127:1 HSCB

He blesses the home of the righteous.
PROVERBS 3:33 NIV

Love each other like brothers and sisters.
Give each other more honor
than you want for yourselves.
ROMANS 12:10 NCV

Above all, put on love—
the perfect bond of unity.
COLOSSIANS 3:14 HCSB

This is My commandment, that you love
one another as I have loved you.
JOHN 15:12 NKJV

More Thoughts About Home and Family

Let your home be your parish, your little
brood your congregation, your living room
a sanctuary, and your knee a sacred alter.

BILLY GRAHAM

Home is the best place to teach young
men and women about God's kind of love.

ELIZABETH GEORGE

It is impossible to overstate the need
for prayer in the fabric of family life.

JAMES DOBSON

A family is a place where principles
are hammered out and honed on
the anvil of everyday living.

CHARLES SWINDOLL

The crown of the home is godliness.

HENRY VAN DYKE

Hold On

(KEEP YOUR HAND ON THE PLOW)
TRADITIONAL SPIRITUAL

Heard the voice of Jesus say,
Come unto me I am the way.
Keep your hand on the plow, hold on.

When my way get dark as night,
I know the Lord will be my light.
Keep your hand on the plow, hold on.

REFRAIN:
Hold on, hold on.
Keep your hand on the plow,
Hold on.

You can talk about me as much as you please,
The more you talk I'm gonna stay on my knees.
Keep your hand on the plow, hold on.

When I get to Heaven gonna sing and shout,
Be nobody there to put me out.
Keep your hand on the plow, hold on.

Don't Give Up!

Let us not become weary in doing good, for at the proper
time we will reap a harvest if we do not give up.
GALATIANS 6:9 NIV

People who live in the country are acutely aware that hard
work pays off and persistence pays, too. So wise country folk rely
less on luck than on elbow grease.

Of course good things do occasionally occur with little or no
effort: Somebody wins the lottery, or inherits a fortune, or stum-
bles onto a financial bonanza by being at the right place at the
right time. But more often than not, good things happen to people
who work hard, and keep working hard when just about everybody
else has gone home or given up.

Calvin Coolidge observed, "Nothing in the world can take
the place of persistence. Talent will not; genius will not; education
will not. Persistence and determination alone are omnipotent."
President Coolidge was right. Perseverance pays big dividends.

If you're enduring tough times, remember that every mara-
thon has a finish line, and so does yours. So keep putting one foot
in front of the other, pray for strength, and don't give up. Whether
you realize it or not, you're up to the challenge if you persevere.
And with God's help, that's exactly what you'll do.

Great accomplishments are often attempted but only
occasionally reached. Those who reach them are
usually those who have missed many times before.
CHARLES SWINDOLL

MORE FROM GOD'S WORD

But as for you, be strong; don't be
discouraged, for your work has a reward.
2 CHRONICLES 15:7 HCSB

We are hard-pressed on every side,
yet not crushed; we are perplexed,
but not in despair.
2 CORINTHIANS 4:8 NKJV

Finishing is better than starting.
Patience is better than pride.
ECCLESIASTES 7:8 NLT

For you have need of endurance,
so that when you have done the will of God,
you may receive what was promised.
HEBREWS 10:36 NASB

So let us run the race that is before us
and never give up. We should remove from
our lives anything that would get in the way
and the sin that so easily holds us back.
HEBREWS 12:1 NCV

WISDOM FROM THE FRONT PORCH

Be like a postage stamp:

stick to one thing till you get there.

JOSH BILLINGS

O How I Love Jesus

FREDERICK WHITFIELD
1855

There is a name I love to hear,
I love to sing its worth.
It sounds like music in my ear,
the sweetest name on earth.

REFRAIN:
O how I love Jesus, O how I love Jesus,
O how I love Jesus, because he first loved me!

It tells me of a Savior's love, who died to set me free;
It tells me of his precious blood, the sinner's perfect plea.

It tells of one whose loving heart can feel my deepest woe;
Who in each sorrow bears a part that none can bear below.

True Disciples

"Follow Me," Jesus told them, "and I will
make you fish for people!" Immediately
they left their nets and followed Him.

MARK 1:17–18 HCSB

Sometimes, it's relatively easy to be a disciple and to proclaim our faith. When we're in the friendly surroundings of our
local church, it's easier to talk about Christ's transforming power
and His never-ending love. But once we've left the security of
the church setting, talking about Jesus can be more difficult.
Nonetheless, God wants us to share His Good News with the
world, witnessing to friends, to family, to casual acquaintances,
and to complete strangers.

As Christians we are called, each in our own way, to share
the story of Jesus. We are commanded to reach out to those in need
and to share the gospel with our communities and with the world.
The need for evangelism is always urgent, and the workers are
always few.

Are you doing your part to share Christ's message? It's a
question only you can answer, and it's a question that you should
answer today.

A disciple is a follower of Christ. That means you take
on His priorities as your own. His agenda becomes
your agenda. His mission becomes your mission.

CHARLES STANLEY

MORE FROM GOD'S WORD

For whoever wants to save his life will
lose it, but whoever loses his life because
of Me and the gospel will save it.
MARK 8:35 HCSB

How happy is everyone who fears the
LORD, who walks in His ways!
PSALM 128:1 HCSB

Follow God's example, therefore,
as dearly loved children.
EPHESIANS 5:1 NIV

Then Jesus spoke to them again: "I am the light
of the world. Anyone who follows Me will never walk
in the darkness, but will have the light of life."
JOHN 8:12 HCSB

Whoever wants to be my disciple must deny
themselves and take up their cross and follow me.
MARK 8:34 NIV

WISDOM FROM THE FRONT PORCH

As we seek to become
disciples of
Jesus Christ,
we should never forget
that the word *disciple* is
directly related to the word
discipline. To be a disciple
of the Lord Jesus Christ
is to know His discipline.

DENNIS SWANBERG

Christ The Lord Is Risen Today

CHARLES WESLEY
1739

Christ the Lord is ris'n today, Alleluia!
Sons of men and angels say, Alleluia!
Raise your joys and triumphs high, Alleluia!
Sing, ye heav'ns, and earth reply, Alleluia!

Love's redeeming work is done, Alleluia!
Fought the fight, the battle won, Alleluia!
Death in vain forbids him rise, Alleluia!
Christ has opened paradise, Alleluia!

Soar we now where Christ has led, Alleluia!
Following our exalted Head, Alleluia!
Made like him, like him we rise, Alleluia!
Ours the cross, the grave, the skies, Alleluia!

King of glory, soul of bliss, Alleluia!
Everlasting life is this, Alleluia!
Thee to know, thy power to prove, Alleluia!
Thus to sing, and thus to love, Alleluia!

He Lives!

He is not here, but He has been resurrected!
LUKE 24:6 HCSB

The tomb could not hold Jesus; on the third day, He rose from the dead. His resurrection is the central event in human history.

Because Jesus lives, His followers are beyond measure. God sent His only Son to die for our sins. We, in turn, should approach our heavenly Father with humility, with reverence, and with thanksgiving. But sometimes amid the crush of our everyday responsibilities, we don't stop long enough to pause and thank our Creator for His blessings.

When we slow down and express our gratitude to the One who made us, we enrich our own lives and the lives of those around us. Thoughtful believers (like you) see the need to praise God with sincerity, with humility, and with consistency. So whatever your circumstances—whether you're sitting on the front porch, or any-where else for that matter—slow down and express your thanks to the Creator. After all, God has given you incalculable gifts, and you owe Him everything, including your eternal gratitude... starting now.

The resurrection of Jesus, the whole alphabet of
human hope, the certificate of our Lord's mission from
heaven, is the heart of the gospel in all ages.
R. G. LEE

MORE FROM GOD'S WORD

On the first day of the week, very early in the
morning, they came to the tomb, bringing the
spices they had prepared. They found the stone
rolled away from the tomb. They went in but
did not find the body of the Lord Jesus.

LUKE 24:1–3 HCSB

Praise be to the God and Father of our Lord
Jesus Christ! In his great mercy he has given
us new birth into a living hope through the
resurrection of Jesus Christ from the dead.

1 PETER 1:3 NIV

For I delivered to you first of all that which I also
received: that Christ died for our sins according
to the Scriptures, and that He was buried, and that
He rose again the third day according to the Scriptures.

1 CORINTHIANS 15:3–4 NKJV

For it is my Father's will that all who see his
Son and believe in him should have eternal
life. I will raise them up at the last day.

JOHN 6:40 NLT

So you also have sorrow now. But I will
see you again. Your hearts will rejoice, and
no one will rob you of your joy.

JOHN 16:22 HCSB

The Resurrection is the biggest news in history. CNN ought to put it on Headline News every thirty minutes. It should scream from every headline:

Jesus is alive!

DENNIS SWANBERG

LIVE YOUR FAITH

Dear Friend,

     This book was prayerfully crafted with you, the reader, in mind—every word, every sentence, every page—was thoughtfully written, designed, and packaged to encourage you...right where you are this very moment. At DaySpring, our vision is to see every person experience the life-changing message of God's love. So, as we worked through rough drafts, design changes, edits and details, we prayed for you to deeply experience His unfailing love, indescribable peace, and pure joy. It is our sincere hope that through these Truth-filled pages your heart will be blessed, knowing that God cares about you—your desires and disappointments, your challenges and dreams.

He knows. He cares. He loves you unconditionally.

BLESSINGS!
THE DAYSPRING BOOK TEAM

**Additional copies of this book and
other DaySpring titles can be purchased
at fine bookstores everywhere.
Order online at dayspring.com
or
by phone at 1-877-751-4347**